Eggs Under
A Red Flag

Ulric Killion

ISBN-10:1466238178

ISBN-13: 978-1466238176

Printed in the United States of America.

Dedication

In Loving Memory of Nina Killion
1937-2006

Loving, caring, and courageous

Contents

Acknowledgements

My loving family and friends made this book possible, which is true of all of my publications. My loving parents, the late Nina Killion and late Maurice Killion, indulged me, especially my loving mother, who seemed to notice at an earlier age my deep inborn curiosity about things of the world and life, which would take me to faraway places. There is the support and advice of my brother, Antonio Killion, and his wife, Annie Killion. My brother is the most honest and courageous person that I have ever personally known, except for my loving mother. There is Lin Rong, whose advice and support has been invaluable. Then there is Antonio Killion, Jr., the artist, who was always ready to lend a helping hand. Finally, there is a special thanks owing to Arion Killion, who is a very young and gifted child that would often inquire about the progress on the book, which motivated me to hurry the book to completion.

Preface

Lin Yutang (1998), in his classic, *My Country and My People*, when making a comparison between Western logic and Chinese logic, wrote, "This brings us to the problem of Chinese logic…" This is because in an earlier era he opines that the opposition of logic versus common sense, essentially, displaced inductive and deductive reasoning. "According to this theory of knowledge," as Lin earlier explained, "truth cannot be proved, although it may be grasped by the mind in a 'dialectic without words (*Chuangtse*),'" which is a sort of intuitive perception.

In the same section of his book, Lin then referred to Bernard Karlgreen's earlier critique concerning "the fallacies of many arguments used by Chinese 'higher critics' in proving the genuineness or spuriousness of ancient works." More importantly, what follows in the same section of the book is Karlgreen's, although arguably intending criticism, marvelous observation about Chinese scholars. According to Lin, Karlgreen observed that Chinese scholars did not write treatises in lengths of five to ten thousand words in order to establish a point, rather they wrote a number of unclassified paragraphs on vast topics and subjects.

Preface

Further, Lin wrote (1998),

> That is why Chinese scholars always bequeath to us so many collections of "notebooks," called *shuipi* or *pichi*, consisting of unclassified paragraphs, in which opinions on the authorship of literary works and corrections of errors in historical records are mixed up with accounts of Siamese twins, fox spirits and sketches of a red-bearded hero or a centipede-eating recluse.

As for the relevance of Lin's words, it is a relevancy that speaks to the writing of this book or, perhaps more accurately, how the book came to full fruition. This is because a book consists of chapters, which are generally the product of preplanning in order to maintain a focus on an overall theme. In this respect, the book is unique because it represents a cumulative process, in that it is the culmination of several essays, which consists of some short essays and some essays longer in length. Uniqueness is also attributable to the fact that the various essays contained in the book were written over a period of about six years. It is a span of years that witnesses some of the essays retaining their original form, while other essays would be subject to change and occasional bouts of re-writing.

Here also lies the greater relevancy of Lin's words, especially about the Chinese scholars from an earlier era. These are the Chinese scholars that would bequeath their collections of notebooks, *shuipi* or *pichi*. It is the description of a cumulative process of writing several essays or articles, which might, if the readers and Chinese scholars will grant indulgence, be befitting of this book. This is because one could say that the book is a cumulative process manifesting a collection of notebooks of "unclassified paragraphs."

Preface

The book, however, is more because although the original form may well constitute a variety of "unclassified paragraphs," over the years a common theme did exist, rather than emerge, and continues to exist, which is the common theme of Chinese culture, the Chinese family system, and the Chinese people.

As for the title of the book, it borrows from the Chinese rock 'n' roll star Cui Jian, the father of Chinese rock 'n' roll, and his 1994 song, *Hongqi Xiade Dan*, which most, in the English language, translate as meaning either eggs under the red flag or balls under the red flag. The book, however, is about neither Cui Jian, nor eggs under the red flag or balls under the red flag.

Nonetheless, there are several reasons for the selection of the title, *Eggs under a Red Flag*, which are also later discussed in Chapter Ten. For instance, the words themselves are implicitly illustrative of Chinese culture, including Chinese history, literature, and other art forms. This is due to very Chinese notions such as "Limited Words (or Characters), but Unlimited Meanings," and the idea that the various art forms are full of hints and suggestions, which require the trained-eye to extrapolate from generalities the specific meanings (Fung, 1991).

Even as regards the title, one must wonder whether these are – limited words, but unlimited meanings. Additionally, one should also wonder whether the words themselves contain certain discoverable meanings from not so obvious hints and suggestions. For instance, the title itself arguably presents an implied-query (i.e., the *petitio principii* or assuming the initial point), which begs the question – so what about Chinese culture, the Chinese family system, and the Chinese people?

All of this also presents issues of interpretations and translations. Notwithstanding the typical problems that associate with language translations, the meanings and

ix

interpretations of many of the topics in the book, including the title, are dependent on and subject to many influences such as race, culture, nationality, and even political preferences. This presents a wide range of possible meanings and interpretations, which could range from the most innocuous meanings and interpretations, to even unspoken sensitivities.

Additionally, the subject matter of Chinese culture is vast, wide, and historical, in that it addresses the spirit or essence of one of the world's oldest civilizations. For this reason, the book explores Chinese culture, the Chinese family system, and the Chinese people by drawing on a diverse and varying range of resources, which range from the old or antiquity, to the new or modernity.

For instance, Chapter One, "Something we do, not something I do," explores Chinese culture by emphasizing the small group phenomenon. It does so by referring to sources dating from Xunzi's (Hsun-tzu, 3rd c. BCE) thoughts (i.e., between the years of 298 and 238 B.C.), to news media sources covering the 2005 arrest of a local official, Lu De Bin, for the murder of his wife.

Chapter Two, "You contain me, I contain you," following the same theme as Chapter One, also addresses these topics by using a wide range of sources that date from the poem written by Madame Kuan, the wife of the artist Chao Mengfu (i.e., Yuan Dynasty, 1271-1368), to a discussion concerning Chinese athletes at the Being 2008 Olympic Games.

Chapter Three, "The Twilight Years – Xu Hang Hong," although following the same theme, shifts attention to the plight of the elderly in China. It does so by generally discussing the retirement of Xiao Mei and her husband, social security, and life after retirement. The chapter also draws on many sources, which range from a famous Russian love song, *Moshike jiawai de wanshang* (1957) (i.e., English translations: "An Evening in Moscow Suburbs," "An evening at

Preface

the suburb of Moscow," or "A night in the suburb of Moscow or Evenings near Moscow"), to recent news media sources concerning the social security of the elderly.

Chapter Four, "Chinese Woman, is Thy Name Frailty," addresses issues of morality (or moralism) and sexism. It does so by shifting the focus of attention to the plight of women or womanhood in both antiquity and modernity. It also does so by referring to diverse sources such as the short film Bus 44 (*Che Si Shi Si*), which was directed by Chinese-American director Dayyán Eng; Shakespeare's writings such as *Hamlet* and *Othello*; and even the *Bible* (i.e., the King James Version).

Then, Chapter Five, "Her Spirit Demoralized," continues the sub-theme of Chapter Four by a greater focus on sources from Chinese history, philosophy, literature, and other art forms. It also does so by referring to diverse sources such as the *Book of Rites* (*Liji*) and the *Liji's Hunyi*; Liu Fu's famous love poem, *Jiao Wo Ruhe Bu Xiang Ta* ("Help me to know how I cannot think of her," 1926); and Zhou En Lai's *About Xian Qi Liang Mu and Duty of Mother* (1942) (*Lun Xianqi Liang Mu Yu Mu Zhi*).

Chapter Six, "Ghosts, Vixens, and 'Fox Spirits,'" which continues the sub-theme of women or womanhood, also employs diverse sources, while also focusing on the tales of ghosts, vixens, and "fox spirits." These sources widely range from the *Yi Jing*, or the *I Ching* (*Book of Changes*); the classic novel of *Fengsheng Yanyi* (*Creation of the Gods*, 1992); the *Shiji* (*The Historical Records*); the classic novel of Pusong Ling (1640-1715), being *Liao Zhai Zhi Yi* (*Fairy Ghost Vixen*); the classic of *Lie Nv Zhuan* (*Collection of Woman Stories*); to the classical poem entitled, *A Plaint of Lady Wang*.

In Chapter Seven, "Lyrics of Lost Love," the book again changes sub-themes by exploring the topic of "lost love" in both antiquity and modernity. The chapter, like earlier chapters, does so by referring to the records and sources of culture. Some of these sources are several poems from the *Shijing* (*Book of Song* or *Book of Odes*); the *Analects of Confucius*; the classic short novel of *Jin Ping Mei*; Ch'ien Chung-shu's book *Wei Cheng* (1942) (*Fortress Beseiged*); and Margaret Mitchell's *Gone with the Wind* (1936). The chapter is entitled, "Lyrics of Lost Love," and commences with an examination of the ideas or ideals of love in antiquity, dating from post-Zhou Chinese culture (or traditional Confucian culture).

Chapter Eight, "The Faces of Ping-Pong," again changes the sub-theme by engaging in a discussion about the sport or even culture of table tennis, ping-pong or *ping-pang*. By doing so, after a discussion of the importance of the sport of ping-pong to the Chinese people, the book intends to relate the importance of ping-pong as being a reflection of Chinese culture, especially the Chinese personality. This is because, for the Chinese people, the sport of ping-pong bears the same cultural significance as, for example, baseball to an America public. Thus, the chapter inevitably explores the many faces of *ping-pang*.

Then, Chapter Nine, "Limited Words, but Unlimited Meanings," turns the reader's attention back to the general theme of culture, including the sub-theme of Chapter Eight. The chapter can be described as a general discussion of about how culture actually works, which is from getting along with others, interacting with local officers, a discussion about why Mao Zedong may have been the master of "fight with the sky, joyful; fight with the land, joyful; fight with people, joyful" (*yu tian dou, qi le wuqiong; yu di dou, qi le wuqiong; yu ren dou, qi le wuqiong*), to simply, "making life" (*weile shenghuo*).

Finally, Chapter Ten, "Just 'Making Life,'" presents a conclusion, which in a summary fashion attempts to address the question – If you ask who the real Chinese people are? This is because the book is about a culture, a family system, and a people that were able to survive disasters and regenerate themselves from one disaster to the next. All of this, ultimately, begs the question – If you ask who the real Chinese people are?

Ulric Killion
June 23, 2011
Shanghai

1

Something we do, not something I do

In terms of Chinese culture, and perhaps a remnant of Chinese traditional culture, the value of a person is an embodiment of society. In modern China, the value of a person remains contingent on the sum total of collective social rules and practices, or the sum of societal rules. What these collective representations convey, according to the late eminent French sociologist Émile Durkheim, the classical social theorist of culture, is the sum total of collective social rules and practices related to the "way the group conceives of itself" (Morrison, 2006; Durkheim, 1938).

As for this hypothetical Chinese person, he is the father, she is the mother, he is the son, she is the daughter, and they are the employers, and other various and more often than not multiple roles. This is because a typical Chinese person, though admittedly somewhat of an abstraction, does not have his/her own personality, in that the personality is not detachable from society and its rules, rather directly related and linked to the same societal rules. Societal residence through the vehicle of social organizations, especial small groups, is crucial. A statement so true that one could conjecture that a person positioning himself or herself outside of society and its social rules (i.e., the collective social rules) will eventually become no more than vanishing vapors; here today, but gone tomorrow.

A person driven by the force of society, and its attendant rules, seeks the shelter of the sanctuary of this force, being society and its rules. It is then that the opportunity for a better job, better pay, and better life reveals itself. Indeed, it is advantageous to succumb to the driving forces of society.

In order to position themselves advantageously, the Chinese people generally need a reference that anchors to society and its rules. If one person has to rely on a reference from another in order to fend for himself or herself, one cannot escape from this force of society. Otherwise, a person will find himself or herself relegated to facing a world alone, rather than under the personality of the phenomenon of small groups and the force of culture and/or traditional culture.

Additionally, the phenomenon of culture or traditional culture is no less an issue of morality or moralism. The words of Xunzi (Hsun-tzu, 3rd c. BCE) lend clearer understanding to this unique variety of moralism. During the pre-Qin confederation of the Zhou (i.e., between the years 298 and 238 B.C.), Xunzi's thoughts are representative of the right wing of the School of Literarti (i.e., the scholars, civil servants, and literati of Imperial China, who were schooled in Confucianism – the School of Literati). For instance, an English translation of one his critical thoughts read, according to Xunzi, "A single individual needs the support of the accomplishments of hundreds of workmen. Yet an able man cannot be skilled in more than one line, and one man cannot hold two offices simultaneously. If people all live alone and do not serve one another, there will be poverty" (Xunzi, 10; Feng, 1952).

In Chinese society, historically, the phenomenon of the small group is pervasive. This is because men and women, though Xunzi was specifically addressing "man," need a social organization. Moreover, in order to form a social organization or small group, rules of conduct are indispensable.

Then there are the nuances of the language attributable to Chinese culture. This is because in Chinese culture, when describing individuals and relationships, the words (or characters) of *ge ren* (individual) and *ge ren* (personality) are rarely used. The exception, though occasionally used in common language usage, occurs when *ge ren* employs not in reference to an individual's personality, rather the personality of a small group.

The language of traditional Confucian culture, which is still persistent and systemic in modern China, also defines a human being by reference to phrases such as "being good" or "being a human being." All of which is also reducible to defining how to handle corresponding relations with others. For example, in Chinese antiquity, there were the relations between the Emperor and *chenzi* (officials subject to the sage-king); a father and son; a husband and wife; brothers; friends; *shu ren* (acquaintances); and even the relations between strangers. The principles of dealing with these various relationships are the core of Chinese traditional culture. In antiquity, these delineated relations were so harsh and compelling that if the Emperor willed the death of a *chenzi*, he must suffer death, and would suffer death.

Lying at the heart of this seeming harshness is fidelity (i.e., *xiao shun*), which required an unconditional obedience to the will and commands of the elder. In modern China, these persistent notions of society via Chinese antiquity, translate into a very practical (or pragmatic) way of life. For instance, at home, "count on parents" (*zai jia kao fumu*); in society, "count on friends" (*chu wai kao pengyou*); and when grow old, "count on children" (*lao le kao zhi nu*). Additionally, the underlying principle of fidelity serves as a guide or even grounding for these pre-determined relations.

For the typical Chinese person, when facing the challenges of family and simply "making life" (*weile shenghuo*), the small group serves as a reference point. In the context of China and Chinese culture, it is a consequence that arises from and attaches to all relevant relations, which includes both relations outside of one's home and inner groups.

For example, there is the study conducted by Jin Wenxue (2004), a Japanese scholar, which is titled, *Koshoku to Chugoku bunka: Chugoku no rekishi wa yoru ni tsukurareta* (i.e., English translations: *Erotic History of China and Chinese culture was made at night* or *Chinese culture and sensuality - Chinese history was made at night*). Jin conducted research, at least in part, regarding the phenomenon of groups in China. While China is a large country, according to Jin (2004), it is more accurate to describe China as a large unit of countless dispensed small groups. These small groups share a certain common interest, because they inevitably compound the interests of individuals.

In the sense of the individual, the latter contention may present a problem for the typical Chinese person, however. This is because the concept of the individual is still wanting in Chinese society, as they remain strongly bound to the concept (or phenomenon) of the group. For this reason,

4

perhaps individualism, if any, presents itself *en masse* via the various small groups.

In Chinese antiquity, the concepts of village or villages, family, and country, also reflected this phenomenon of the group or small groups. This is due to early society actually comprising small villages. The birth of the small village was the nucleus of the Chinese family, or simply, the family or kindred (*jiaju*). The formation of these small villages routinely entailed the construction of a fortress wall. As a means of protection from enemies, these small communities also invariably built, or dug, a river alongside these small communities. As night fell, there was the daily closing of the village gate to the wall. Determining who was an enemy was a relatively easy task, because enemies remained outside the walls, while friends were safe inside or within the walls. It was quite easy to determine who was bad or good.

Conceptually, in antiquity these small communities manifested large families, self-contained groups or small groups. In the Chinese language, *guo jia* means country. However, it is important to understand the etymology of the phrase *guo jia*. For instance, *guo* taken alone means country, while *jia* taken alone means family. In traditional Chinese culture (or traditional Confucianism), the framework of a country is that of a family. For this reason, arguably, the principles or rules governing how to maintain both a country and a family are identical.

In modern China, one can still witness the same phenomenon appearing in many aspects of life. For instance, even on college campuses this pervasive concept of groups or small-groups is also at work. On Chinese college campuses, the formation of their social groups or small groups arise by virtue of similar dialects and the region of origins of students, such as students hailing from the same towns and speaking the same local dialects. This is quite different from

Western college campuses, where they generally form social relations or social groups just because they all like something, or have some common interest such as a hobby, sports or a course of study such as engineering.

Conversely, the Chinese social groups or small groups on campuses reveal a motivation by the students to want to help one another, take care of each other, and stay in close contact with each other. A primary motivation of these social groups on Chinese campuses is a "survival in groups" instinct, rather than a Western variety of social acceptance such as popularity. Chinese society is a group-oriented society. For instance, those living abroad also tend to develop social groups and organizations based on a common Chinese heritage. In China, every person from every class, occupation, and lifestyle feels some degree of instability and stress. In order to "make life," people have to form a network, in order to take care of each other. Practically speaking, this is the core of the social network.

Social networks can sometimes manifest unstable relationships, however. This is because in real life these networks may be strong or weak, or even vacillate between being strong and weak. Social networks stem from the family, common interests, and even potential interests. These relationships can be very long in duration, very short, or even very strong or loose-knit. All of which depends on the nature of the common interests of the various social relations, social groups, social networks or small groups.

In the language nuances of Chinese culture, people are either inside or outside of the various social relations, social groups, social networks or small groups. For instance, people deemed inside or belonging to a social network enjoy the characterization of being *shu ren* (acquaintances), while those who are outside or do not belong to a social network are *sheng ren* (strangers).

As for the etymology of these terms, *shu* generally means, "well done," while *sheng* denotes "uncooked." It is notable that these social network characterizations or the attributive adjectives of *shu* and *sheng* normally associate with the preparation of food for a meal. In many respects, all social networks relate to having a meal, such as people sharing Chinese dishes or being together in a small group enjoying hot pot (*huo guo*). As previously mentioned, the members of the social network are the *shu ren*, and these are the people you will see from the smallest village to the largest city in group gatherings in crowded restaurants enjoining family, friends, and Chinese cuisine.

In China, crowded restaurants are a commonplace activity of daily life, even in the very small cities or villages. In some of the larger cities, even some restaurants resemble hotels, because these restaurants have four or five floors for dining with large banquet size tables. This is because for doing business, the Chinese people will normally want to discuss business matters during a meal or dinner, and sometimes may even conclude contract negotiations after an evening of drinks and dinner. In these surroundings, friends, family, and business associates meet each other, especially in the winter months.

The Chinese people especially enjoy going to have hot pot with friends, family, and business associates, because the routine of having hot pot is sitting around a table visiting, while watching the food cook before your eyes. Around the hot pot table, they enjoy different kinds of food and beverages, and you can see the excitement in their faces, as they persuade each other in loud voices to drink. The Chinese network works like the net of a spider, because it matters not who he or she is or whether one lives in a poor village or rich villa, persons inside the network share their moments of happiness and difficulties.

As earlier mentioned, the phenomenon of the group can sometimes also manifest unstable relationships, which often produces shocking consequences for Chinese society. For instance, on June 17, 2005, the *He Nan Ribao* (*Henan Daily*) reported the criminal wrongdoing of Lu De Bin, who was then vice provincial governor of Henan province. Notwithstanding he was a vice provincial governor, following reforms commenced in the 1980s, he was one of the first Chinese students to be sent abroad to study. Lu went abroad to the United State and successfully pursued post-graduates studies or a PhD degree in the field of agriculture. Despite past successes and achievements, having to face a charge of murder in the public eye presented an unprecedented turn in the life of Lu De Bin.

Although the arrest of Lu for the murder of his wife is shocking in and of itself, another shocking aspect of his crime is that he hired someone else to murder his wife. According to a June 18, 2005 Singapore newspaper account of the crime, the *Xin Ming Daily*, Lu de Bin, in order to have his wife murdered, asked a vice-mayor in his province to find someone who would murder his wife. The vice-mayor then sought the assistance of a local police officer, who found the two persons that actually murdered his wife and cut her body into pieces.

The case of Lu De Bin is shocking in several respects. First, the murder involved several officers of the local government. Second, Lu's position of status, in conjunction with his educational accomplishments, also lent to the shocking aspects of the crime. Third, this incident demonstrates the potency of the social network, especially the possible negative aspects of the phenomenon of social networks or small groups in China.

Quoting from one of Feng Menglong's Chinese classics, which is from the story about The Beggar Chief's Daughter, in *The Courtesan's Jewel Box* (Feng, 1981),

> *A loyal man wins praise throughout his life,*
> *But cursed be he who spurns a loving wife!*
> *A murdered wife may come to life again:*
> *So all attempts to thwart the gods are vain!*

Nonetheless, a strongly woven social network enables Lu to procure the death of his wife by murder via the vehicle of his social network. It was through his social network that he sought an answer to a seemingly simple problem concerning his wife, such as simply obtaining a divorce. Lu relied on friends or *shu ren*, who are those inside the social network to help him with his marital problems by murdering his wife.

Due to the Lu De Bin case and other similar instances, some Chinese people are beginning to think they are becoming a cold people. There are many examples that illustrate what many deem to be increasingly cold and rude manners or behavior in public such as some people pushing and shoving their way through the aisle of a bus, and failing to lend assistance to the victim of a robbery.

In anticipation of the Beijing 2008 Olympics Games, local authorities were seeking to address what they deem uncivilized behavior such as rudeness, spitting, and littering through the vehicle of an official etiquette watchdog, the Spiritual Civilization Steering Committee of the Chinese Communist Party. For example, on May 8, 2007, the *China Daily* reported that pursuant to this campaign to cultivate courtesy and civility, the 11th day of each month is designed "voluntarily wait in line" day, which is designed to stamp out pushing and shoving in favor of orderly queues.

Perhaps the main reason for what seems an increase in intolerable behavior is Chinese culture, especially the concepts of inside and outside the social network. This is because the Chinese people treat people or *shu ren*, who are those "inside" their social networks, like family or friends, because *shu ren* are very friendly. They are family and friends and seem to have no boundaries between them, except when they become too involved in the lives of others. There is also the questionable behavior or rude behavior such as spitting in public and throwing garbage out of a window. It is a different issue at home for most of the Chinese people, however, because while within the confines of their homes, they generally maintain very neat and clean premises. Perhaps another example of the inside and outside dichotomy is that they generally treat those "inside" well, but not those that are "outside".

Lin Yutang earlier made an astonishing observation about what he characterizes as the indifference of the Chinese people. As Lin (1998) earlier opined,

> I think this indifference is not a natural characteristic of the people, but is a conscious product of our culture, deliberately inculcated by our old-world wisdom under the special circumstances. Taine once said that vice and virtue are products like sugar and vitriol. Without taking such an absolute view, one can nevertheless subscribe to the general statement that any virtue will be more generally encouraged in a society where that virtue is easily seen to be

"good," and is more likely to be generally accepted as part of life.

Moreover, according to Lin, the Chinese people generally acquire this indifference from experience and as a means of survival. Further, Lin (1998) wrote,

> The Chinese people take to indifference as Englishmen take to umbrellas, because the political weather always looks a little omnious for the individual who ventures a little too far out alone, in other words, indifference has a distinct "survival value" in China. Chinese youth are as public-spirited as foreign youths, and Chinese hot-heads show as much desire to "meddle with public affairs" as those in any other country. But somewhere between their twenty-fifth and their thirtieth years, they all become wise (*"hsueh kaui liao,"* as we say), and acquire this indifference which, contributes a lot to their mellowness and culture. Some learn it by native intelligence, and others by getting their fingers burned once or twice. All old people play safe because all old rogues have learned the benefits of indifference in a society where personal rights are not guaranteed and one's fingers burned once is bad enough.

Additionally, modern China is experiencing tremendous domestic issues, especially concerning the social security of its citizens, but the Chinese people always manage to interject some degree of stability into their lives. All are in search of a stable life, and the root of this wished for stability comes to fruition through Chinese culture, the Chinese family system, and the Chinese people themselves. The Chinese family system is a source of solace and relaxation from stress, which also enables the regeneration of lost hopes. It is akin to the feeling of having someone at home waiting with a warm light in hand, which is same aura of life that keeps people struggling for their families.

Most Chinese people use this simple philosophy to help get them through tough times, no matter who he or she is, such as farmers, government officers or officials, and scholars. Demonstrating the critical importance of the family, the Chinese people have a saying, which is *shang you lao, xia you xiao* (we have elder, we have children). Young and old, and the most creative of mind, all seem to follow the advice of mother and wives to avoid trouble. Maybe because of this emphasis on family, no matter what kind of reforms they have lived through, people still use this simple philosophy to "make life" (*weile shenghuo*), and to sustain Chinese culture for generations to come.

2

You contain me,
I contain you

During the period from 1200-1300, or the 13th century, which is during the Yuan Dynasty (*Yuan chao*, 1271-1368), the wife of an artist penned a poem. The artist was the Yuan painter Chao Mengfu, and his wife was Madame Kuan, who was also a painter and teacher at the Imperial Court. An English translation of the poem follows (Jin, 2011).

Twixt you and me
There's too much emotion.
That's the reason why
There's such a commotion!
Take a lump of clay,
Wet it, pat it,
And make an image of me,
And an image of you.
Then smash them, crash them,

And add a little water.
Break them and re-make them,
Into an image of you,
And an image of me,
Then in my clay, there's a little of you,
And in your clay, there's a little of me.
And nothing ever shall we sever;
Living, we'll sleep in the same quilt,
And dead, we'll be buried together.

Madame Kuan originally penned the poem because her husband, Chao Mengfu, had decided to take a concubine. The taking of a concubine, or young girl, was a generally acceptable social practice for men of this period as they approached middle age. Madame Kuan seeking to discourage her husband wrote this poem intending to sway her husband from taking a concubine. The importance of the poem also owes to Madame Kuan's unique analogy of the mixing of clay and water in describing the relationship of marriage between a man and a woman.

In the context of Chinese history and literature, this is the first instance of the clay and water analogy appearing in literature. As for the symbolic significance, the analogy actually intends to serve as a symbol of marriage. This symbolic significance arises from the idea that the husband is clay and the wife is water. Moreover, when you begin the processes of kneading and re-kneading a mixture of clay and water, the water permeates clay and then molds clay. Following the permeation and molding of clay, the clay now holding water is able to give substance to the water, which now allows the water to move, live, and come into full being.

You contain me, I contain you

Additionally, the wonder of the story behind this poem is that she was successful in doing so, because the poem did move Chao Mengfu, as he cancelled his plan to have a concubine. One could say that Madame Kuan's famous poem is about the sentimentalism of her era, which addresses those shared feelings that people will normally experience. Couples, family members, and friends, all share some experiences and memories. Most of which are shared similar experiences and memories, which also means there is normally not a strong borderline between family members and friends.

For the Chinese people, if there does exists a borderline, it probably relates to the concept of the individual or individualism. The latter typically manifests in the elders, parents, and friends often using the phraseology of "for your own good." Accordingly, for their own good, there are many decisions and plans made for family and friends, including their children, which consequently means greater involvement in the lives of others and controlling the lives of others.

For instance, if you ever have the experience of dining with Chinese people, you will observe that they use their *kuaizi* (chopsticks) to give their guest and children food. The Chinese people understand this kindness of welcoming their family and friends or *shu ren* by this simple demonstration of caring for others. However, sometimes your food can become my poison, because, in some instances, some may perceive this simple display of kindness as an act akin to a hard sell. Food can become poison when one tries to push their personal views on others, which implicitly may constitute a denial of the judgments of others. One can count many of these instances in the daily lives of the Chinese people.

Eggs under a Red Flag

Every summer in China, and throughout the country, the government conducts the annual three-day college admission examinations. The government by now convening these examinations in the month of July, rather than in June, may arguably demonstrate the importance of these examinations. In China, the dates of June 7, June 8, and June 9 are now common knowledge and events to everyone, so as each yearly round of examinations approach, you can observe the tension in many parents. There are even incidents of suicide by parents associated with the stress attendant to these examinations, because parents, whether right or wrong, associate their "face" (i.e., *mian zi* and/or *zhun lian*) with the performance of their child or children.

It is a level of stress associated with the parent's "face," which is so stressful that many parents wish they could stand in the shoes of their child and take the examination for them. This high level of stress inevitably affects both the parents and students, because the only seeming outlet for this stress is a successful test result and subsequent admission to a state university. Beginning as early as the elementary school level, as Pamela Phan (2005; Alford and Fang, 1994) explained in her study of the educational system, "Chinese students are expected to learn through a system the Chinese call "stuffing the duck" (*tianya shi*), cramming facts, figures, and theories into hours of classroom lectures, followed by hours of memorization at home."

The World Olympics provides another illustration, because during the Beijing 2008 Olympic Games there were several interesting occurrences. The American participants (or athletes) appeared to enjoy their matches, because for them the stadium was like a stage. For the American participants or athletes being in front of a camera was like being under the lights of a stage. This was their chance to display not only their skills, but also their personalities.

A prime example is the flamboyant National Basketball Association (NBA) star Dennis Rodman, who on August 13, 2011 during his induction to the Hall of Fame speech, humbly let everyone know "that his act was just that – an act" (Mahoney, 2011).

From a Chinese perspective, however, these American athletes were exhibiting behavior similar to that, for instance, of an American National Football League (NFL) football player that after scoring a touchdown performs a touchdown dance ritual. The American athlete, like the NFL football player who scores a touchdown, appears to want to just show off by an exhibition or display of his individual personality traits, rather than a more serious commitment to the game, such as wearing different hairstyles.

In comparison, the Chinese participant in the World Olympics is different. Because he or she bears the expectations of the country, society, coaches, leaders, teammates, friends, parents, and family. While patriotism motivates the American athletes, the Chinese athlete carries an added burden that often results in an inability to experience the simple joy of sports competition, which seems more so experienced by an American athlete. For the Chinese athlete, admittedly, the expectations intend to obtain a good result or victory in competition. However, there is a price paid for these expectations, which is the resulting stress, rather than experience of pure enjoyment of the competition or games.

In the 2004 Olympics, during a diving competition, which is one of China's favorite games, a young male diver fell off the board, scoring zero points. The leaders of the diving team thought that he had lost "their face," while the leaders of the state teams, who are over all of the teams participating, also thought that he lost "their face." Having scored zero, on the same night, the young diver's coach had him write a paper describing what happened, while also spending the night thinking about what had happened. The latter was hardly an experience conducive to enhancing performance, rather one enhancing the stress of competition.

The incident involving the young diver at the Olympics is similar to the incidents involving parents and children or students during the annual state college admission examinations. Irrespective of the age of students and athletes, the coaches, leaders, teachers, and parents actually treat the athletes and students as if they are were still children. The coaches, leaders, and parents feel they have more responsibility than the actual students and athletes in the stadiums, classrooms, and examination rooms.

In China, the status of legal divorces presents another illustration, because the parents of married-couples treat both parties to a marriage or a divorce as *bu xiao shun*. This is because, in the event of a divorce, parents feel that the children have lost "their face," which is the "face" of the parents, rather than the children. In China, a group of unhappily married couples were polled regarding why they did not seek a divorce, and they generally responded that they have parents and they have children, or *shang you lao, xia you xiao* (we have parents, we have children), how can we explain divorce to them? Some Chinese people simply relegate their own feelings to a secondary status in respect of others, being country, society, leaders, coaches, teachers, family, and friends.

Moreover, even the simple event of a meal demonstrates this same idea. For instance, throughout the world many recognize and enjoy Chinese food. Everyone who has enjoyed genuine Chinese cuisine will understand that these foods comprise different ingredients such as vegetables, meats, sauces, and other food items. Different ingredients are prepared in one dish, and during these marvelous cooking processes, each ingredient penetrates and blends with the others to produce a distinctive Chinese cuisine enjoyed throughout the world.

In this respect, each ingredient is separate, but becomes a part of the other ingredients, and as a result each ingredient will contain a part (or a taste or flavor) of the other ingredients. It is also like the Western cuisine of the salad, which comprises different ingredients such as vegetables, meats, fruits, and other food items. The separable items once blended together make a colorful dish, and contribute their own personalities (or taste and flavor) and even colors.

Moreover, on the subject of the Chinese people and food, as Lin Yutang (1993) earlier explained,

> It there is anything we are serious about, it is neither religion nor learning, but food. We openly acclaim eating as one of the few joys of this human life. This question of attitude is very important, for unless we are honest about it we will never be able to lift eating and cooking into an art. The difference of attitude regarding the problem of food is represented in Europe by the French and the English. The French eat enthusiastically, while the English eat apologetically. The Chinese national genius decidedly leans toward the French in the matter of feeding ourselves.

In the final analysis, "you contain me, I contain you." The children, now adults and unhappily married, cannot simply obtain a divorce just because of their feelings and thoughts. They must seriously consider the parents and their children. It is no less different from the athletes striving to participate in the Olympics and young Chinese students aspiring to admission to Chinese state universities. Because they are unable to simply ignore the expectations of coaches, leaders, teachers, friends, and family. In Chinese society, "you contain me, I contain you."

3

The Twilight Years –
Xu Hang Hong

As of December 2010, according to official data, the number of Chinese Communist Party (CCP) members, though some argue the high count is only bravado for the CCP's 90th anniversary, rose to 80.27 million members.[1] Do all of these members believe in communism? Most of these members, actually, seek acceptance in mainstream society. They want to belong to a group, which may be needs based on psychological needs, rather than a belief in party ideology. The average Chinese person actually has little, if any, knowledge of communist ideology, including Marxism.

A primary concern of the average Chinese citizen is simply how to "make life." In other words, the primary issues of taking care of one's family, friends, or their inner groups or

---

[1] The Communist Party of China (CPC, CCP), ChinaToday.com; http://www.chinatoday.com/org/cpc/.

small groups. Perhaps even a question of survival or a variety of survival earlier mentioned in Chapter One, which characterizes the notion of a "survival in groups" instinct. Thus, the decision whether to join the CCP will necessarily link to issues of how best to "make life."

For example, there is the story of Xiao Mei. During the long hours of an air flight crossing the Pacific Ocean from Chicago, to Shanghai, she related a story of life in China and retirement in China. She and her husband were lifelong members of the CCP. Both of them worked as schoolteachers in the public school system. She worked at an elementary school teaching math, and her husband worked at a public university teaching chemistry. When we met, she was 60 years of age and her husband was 70 years of age. They married in 1958 and as life partners they would witness many changes in modern China.

After a full life of having both taught school and raised a family, they found themselves having to adjust to the fact of retirement. Xiao Mei mentioned the day a local official informed her of her pending retirement, which became effective in 2005. In China, the legal retirement ages for men and women are different and, by law, are now 55 years of age for women and 60 years of age for men. In 2005, according to Fu Jing (2005), China's Ministry of Labor and Social Security had forecasted that the number of retired person living in urban areas will increase to about 70 million in 2010, and then to about 100 million by 2020. In urban areas, as of 2005, there were about 48 million persons of pension age, but only 44.9 percent of them were urban employees and 85.4 percent of retired persons were covered by pension plans, while most farmers were ineligible or outside of the pension system (Killion, 2006; *China Daily*, December 15, 2005; Fu, 2005).

The Twilight Years – Xu Hang Hong

Xiao Mei recalled the exact day and month of this event, because the anticipated retirement date would pose a certain problem in her life. It was no less different for her husband when he retired, although she indicates that she adjusted relatively well to the announcement he would also have to retire. On the date the officer announced that she would have to retire, she went home and wept alone. Sadness consumed her during this period. She suffered a sadness that would have been unbearable without the support of her family and friends. Xiao Mei was not ready for the *xu hang hong* – the red sunset.

After her last day at work, she suffered from depression, or what she described as *qingxu di luo* (depressed). In the days that followed, when she met someone, she always inquired whether he or she knew where she could find a new job. She would have worked regardless of a high or low salary, and even without pay. She still wanted to work, because work had always been an important part of her life. Although she had a relatively decent pension, especially when compared to other retirees, she simply wanted to work. The loss of her job left an empty void in her life.

Before the mandatory retirement, Xiao Mei and her husband did not really have hobbies. However, after retirement, she would eventually find herself frequenting a club of retired teachers. The club provided a great relief from her loss of a job. At the club, she could sing with the others members, dance, and take part in trips to other provinces. As for her husband and his retirement, he had earlier joined a sports team, which was a croquette club, and had even attended drawing classes. Xaoi Mei said that she gradually make a successful transition to her new life.

The crisis felt by Xiao Mei upon hearing the announcement that her retirement was impending arguably could have been less stressful with the strength offered through prayer and faith. Most Chinese people, however, do not believe in religion, in the sense of Western Christianity. As observed by Derk Bodde (1946),

> They [the Chinese] are not people for whom religious ideas and activities constitute an all-important and absorbing part of life ... It is ethics (especially Confucian ethics), and not religion (at least not religion of a formal organized type), that provided the spiritual basis in Chinese civilization ... All of which, of course, marks a difference of fundamental importance between China and most other major civilizations, in which a church and priest have played a dominant role.

In the context of China, when people retire, and their children have already left home, like Xiao Mei's sons, who studied and now live abroad, they suffer from the feeling of having lost the supporting fulcrum for their lives, perhaps even a sense of having lost themselves. However, Chinese people seem adept at adjusting to changes in life or getting this fulcrum of life back. If you ever have a chance to visit China, you should visit one of the many crowded public parks in Chin such as *Lu Xun Gongyuan* (Lu Xun Public Park) in Shanghai; *Yue Xiu Gongyuan* (Yue Xiu Public Park) in Guangzhou, Guangdong Province; or *Bei Hai Gongyuan* (Bei Hai Public Park) in Beijing.

There is much to see at these public gatherings, which comprise the old and young and many events. If you were to visit one of the public park gatherings, you will observe that the elders are very active participants in various activities. For instance, there are many spontaneous activities of the elders such as *Tai ji* (or *Chai ji*).

They also join in the singing of songs that were popular during their youth, and many of these songs are Russian love songs and folk songs. A prime example is Vasily Solovjev-Sedoi's 1955 Russian love song, though the words were written by Mikhail Matusovsky, entitled *Moshike jiawai de wanshang* (i.e., English translations: "An Evening in Moscow Suburbs," "An evening at the suburb of Moscow," "A night in the suburb of Moscow" or "Evenings near Moscow"). An English translation of the first verse of *Moshike jiawai de wanshang* reads as follows.

Out on my own
In the suburbs of Moscow
Out in the rain
Walking down this long avenue

Out to the crowds in the square
Feelings are high everywhere

But the feeling is gone
And I can't break away
(living in Moscow)
Out in the cold
(so cold)
When there is nowhere to stay

This famous Russian love song, "*Moshike jiawai de wanshang*," would subsequently (i.e., post-1955) serve as a symbol of both the 1957 Youth Festival in Moscow, and then later, Nikita Khruschev (1894-1971) easing the constraints of social-political life in the Russian heartland. The fondness of the Chinese people, especially the older generation, for this Russian love song may serve as a reminder of an earlier parallel between social-political life in the Russian heartland, or Soviet Union, during the 1950s and 1960s, and that of social-political life in China during the same periods.

Another example is the Russian love story entitled *Ao bao xiang hui* (i.e., English translations: "Meeting in Aobao," "Meeting in the Mongolian Tent," or "The 15th Moon"). For instance, a language translation from Chinese to English of the latter song, *Ao bao xiang hui*, follows.

> *Shi wu de yue liang sheng shang liao tian kong na*
> *Wei shen me pang bian mei you yun cai*
> *Wo deng dai zhe mei li de gu niang yani*
> *Wei shen me hai bu dao lai yo he*

The moon on the fifteenth rises into the sky
Why are there no clouds on the side?
I am waiting for a beautiful girl
Why have you still not yet arrived?

-

> *Ruo guo mei you tian shang de yu shui ya*
> *Hai tang hua er bu hui zi ji kai*
> *Zhi yao ge ge wo nai xin deng dai yo*
> *Wo xin shang de ren er jiu hui guo lai yo he*

The Twilight Years – Xu Hang Hong

> If there is no rainwater in the sky
> the cherry-apple blossoms won't bloom by themselves.
> Older brother, as long as I wait patiently
> the person on my heart will arrive.

There are also locals performing Chinese Beijing operas such as *Su shan qi jie*. Then there are the bouts of contest such as Chinese chess, *Ma Jiang*, and even the ancient Chinese board game of *Go* (or *Weiqi*). One has to witness personally these public park gatherings in order to feel both the excitement and warmth of the people as they spend their afternoons in these public parks.

Confucius once said, *Lao you shuo yang* (the elders must be taken care of). This early Confucian thought typifies modern examples of old ideas, the old ways, and the traditions in antiquity, if any, that are still prevalent in modern society. As Xiao Mei and her husband would eventually turn to their friends and family or social groups in dealing with their late life circumstances, because the state simply retires them and gives them an adequate pension. In real life, however, what their family, friends, and social groups were able to provide them, the state would never be able to match. From the help of friends, family, and their social groups, Xiao Mei addresses her problem of depression (*qingxu di luo*) and the loss of her job, like the Chinese students on college campuses, by finding other persons, especially other elderly persons that just want to help one another, take care of each other, and stay in close contact with each other.

In the end, for Xiao Mei and her husband, the "survival in groups" instinct once again enables them to simply "make life." For the same reason, it was not a flag or song such as a Russia folk song or an impromptu singing of a red song commemorating the birth of the CCP, which, in and of themselves, enables them to get back the fulcrum of life back, or simply, once again "make life." Xiao Mei and her husband, like others, sing the old Russian folk songs or even red songs for the simple joy of relaxation, being with others, and sharing moment of life with family and family, their social groups, or simply, their *shu ren* (acquaintances).

Chinese Woman, is Thy Name Frailty

The chapter begins with an introduction to the 2002 short film "Bus 44" (*Che Si Shi Si*). It is a short film, which is only about eleven minutes in duration, and directed by Chinese-American director Dayyán Eng. The short film "Bus 44" is immediately distinguishable as the first Chinese language short film for both its selection and subsequent awards at several film festivals. It is the first Chinese language short film to win an award at the Venice Film Festival, Sundance Film Festival, Florida Film Festival, Cannes Film Festival, and Hong Kong Film Festival.

Reviewers praised this short film as great, with beautiful cinematography, especially its winter sceneries of China. Reviewers also found this short-film to be complete, and admired it as a self-restraint on the part of the director not to turn this short piece into a longer one. Reviewers, also while finding the short film was well paced and intriguing, defied anyone not to react to the underlying message of the movie.

As for the background setting in "Bus 44," there is a female bus driver, a public bus, villains and a hero, China's countryside, and the countryside road that winds around a mountain. The storyline of the short film evolves around what would normally be a routine bus trip in the countryside, but turns into a horrible tragedy.

The short film starts with the routine of a female public bus driver, which is a role that the actor Gong Beibei plays, on a bus route that travels deserted countryside roads. While driving her rural bus route, the bus driver stops on a countryside road to pick up a young male passenger, which is a role that the actor Wu Chao plays. The young man boards bus 44 and has a brief exchange with the attractive driver, but she does not show any interest in his conversation so he takes a seat on the bus.

What next occurs is a series of tragedies, beginning with two highway robbers hijacking the bus and robbing the passengers of their money. This is only the beginning of this tragic storyline, because after robbing the passengers, the two robbers dragged the bus driver off the bus and then behind some nearby bushes, where they proceed to rape her violently, which is a gruesome and difficult aspect of the film to watch. During the violent rape of the bus driver, only one passenger - the young man - tries to save her, while the others passengers do what many innocent bystanders seem to do, which is "do nothing." This is not the end of the storyline or series of tragedies, however, because as the bus drives off with the now bemused young man, there is another twist or tragedy in the storyline.

After the tragic rape scene, and one still wonders why such a gruesome scene was necessary, the robbers took the bus driver back to the bus and let her resume driving the bus. At this point, the bus driver tells the young man, who tried to save her, that he must get off the bus. The young man responded no, and that he was trying to save her. She responded you tried to save me, but what did you save? He said that even though I could not save you, I have a ticket and a right to be on your bus. She then said rudely to him that if he did not get off the bus, she would not drive the bus.

Surprisingly, the earlier quiet passengers, who did not attempt to help the bus driver, now offered their assistance. They did so by telling the young man that he had better get off the bus because they have many things to take care of in town, and do not waste our time. The robbers also lent a hand by throwing the young man's luggage out of a bus window, and shoving him off the bus. With the young man no longer aboard, the driver resumes driving the bus down a countryside road.

The bus started a climb up a steep country road, and as it approached the top of mountain, with the left side of the road being the mountain and the right side being a dangerous drop from the mountain. As the bus drove around a curve on this steep mountain, the bus driver accelerated the speed of the bus. One of the robbers realized that something was wrong and started yelling at her to slow down and what are you doing? The bus driver failed to respond and only drove faster. One of the robbers then tries to take the steering wheel from her, but he was too late, because the bus driver veered the bus to the right side of the road, and then off the mountain.

The following day a local newspaper reported that somewhere in the mountain area of our town there was a disaster. A public bus went off the mountain and eleven passengers, together with the bus driver, are all dead. As for the young man, when he first read this newspaper account his immediate response was joy, shown by a smile on his face. However, the smile turned to sadness as he continues to read the newspaper account, while crying.

The point of the short film seems centered on the consequence that only one man, being the young man that boarded the public bus and attempted to chat with her, attempted to stop the robbers, while watching her suffer the tragedy of a violent rape. Supposedly, from the director's perspective, this incident serves as an example of a universal ideal that transcends boundaries and societies, and demonstrates the best and worst of human behavior or human nature. It also leaves one wondering, what importance the director attributed to the female bus driver in this short film.

This storyline of this short film bears mentioning for a reason. It demonstrates that the records of history or culture, as expressed in conventional forms of art are, at least partially, reflected and influenced by the many viewpoints of writers, artists, painters, poets, and playwrights. In China, these writers, artists, painters, poets, and playwrights are predominately men in both antiquity and modernity, all of which record history from their point of view, which has always been a predominately-male point of view.

In "Bus 44," the director also arguably shows the world a poor image of China, connoting that it is unsafe place and how cruel they Chinese people are. However, and problematic, is that the director arguably treated the female bus driver as nothing more than background for his movie, and no different than the public bus that veered down the steep mountain slope. Perhaps the development of Chinese culture is a history of a manipulative culture, especially concerning the development of women. This is because the bus driver may have been a mother, a wife, a daughter, or a sister, but from the short film, we can only see and know that she has tears in her eyes.

However, prior to judging the Chinese people and the status of women in both antiquity and modernity, we should first look to Western society for a possible standard and morality concerning women. Because once the West itself does so, it may be less inclined to judge China and the state of womanhood overly harsh. Assuming the arts or art forms of a society truly reflect culture, cultural forms, and cultural values, we should first look to William Shakespeare (1564 - 1616), who many experts hail as the greatest English dramatist and poet. Shakespeare, in *Hamlet* (Shakespeare, 2007), wrote, "Frailty, thy name is woman." These Shakespearean words make one wonder, Chinese woman what is your name? Is the name for Chinese women, the same as that for other women hailing from other places, especially the West?

From Shakespeare's words or writings, we can arguably sense a degree of paternalism, perhaps even a sense of protectiveness towards women. The great bard wrote these words, being "Frailty, thy name is woman," during the 16th century, which may or may not speak well for his generation, and possibly the generations of Western society that followed.

Moreover, the words spoken to Ophelia are harsh and belittling. Hamlet sees a weak and fail woman in her. Shakespeare by his choice of words intends to make her so, which is a seemingly weak and frail woman. Ophelia is also an obedient and dependent woman, as shown by her dependence on her father when she is cruel to Hamlet, although she loves him. The latter dependence on her father and arguably cruelty is demonstrated when she allows her father to use her to spy on Hamlet, the man she loves. An excerpt from Shakespeare's *Hamlet* (Shakespeare, 2007) that contains this passage follows.

> Hyperion to a satyr; so loving to my mother,
> That he might not beteem the winds of heaven
> Visit her face too roughly. Heaven and earth!
> Must I remember? Why, she would hang on him
> As if increase of appetite had grown
> By what it fed on: and yet, within a month,--
> Let me not think on't,--Frailty, thy name is woman!—
> A little month; or ere those shoes were old
> With which she followed my poor father's body
> Like Niobe, all tears;--why she, even she,--
> O God! a beast that wants discourse of reason,
> Would have mourn'd longer,--married with mine uncle,
> My father's brother; but no more like my father…

In Shakespeare's words, one can sense a strong person, a strong man, and maybe even a man of feelings with a heart, who is, indeed, a sensitive and full person. His attitude toward women was arguably sympathy and fondness. Shakespeare, however, has forever been the subject of controversy and dissension.

There are two sides to Shakespeare. One side is the image of being the greatest writer in the English language. In accordance with this image, one can return to *Hamlet*, and find the often-quoted words "Get thee to a nunnery." The latter is subject to a perhaps paternalistic Shakespeare, through the vehicle of *Hamlet*, seeking to soundly advise, or bid, Ophelia to go to a nunnery where she can live a life of celibacy. An excerpt from *Hamlet*, Act 1, Scene 1, containing this passage follows.

> HAMLET
> Ha, ha! Are you honest?
> OPHELIA
> My lord?
> HAMLET
> Are you fair?
> OPHELIA
> What means your lordship?
> HAMLET
> That if you be honest and fair, your honesty should admit no discourse to your beauty.
> OPHELIA
> Could beauty, my lord, have better commerce than with honesty?
> HAMLET
> Ay, truly; for the power of beauty will sooner transform honesty from what it is to a bawd than the force of honesty can translate beauty into his likeness. This was sometime a paradox, but now the time gives it proof. I did love you once.
> OPHELIA
> Indeed, my lord, you made me believe so.
> HAMLET
> You should not have believed me, for virtue cannot so inoculate our old stock but we shall relish of it. I loved you not.
> OPHELIA
> I was the more deceived.
> HAMLET

> Get thee to a nunnery. Why wouldst thou be a breeder of sinners? I am myself indifferent honest, but yet I could accuse me of such things that it were better my mother had not borne me: I am very proud, revengeful, ambitious, with more offences at my beck than I have thoughts to put them in, imagination to give them shape, or time to act them in. What should such fellows as I do crawling between earth and heaven? We are arrant knaves all; believe none of us. Go thy ways to a nunnery. Where's your father?

Then, there is the other side of Shakespeare. According to British lecturer Robert Williams, he is one of the most offensive writers, declaring, "His vulgarity makes Howard Stern seem like Mr. Rogers" (Foster, 2005). In illustrating his point, Williams uses Hamlet's advice to Ophelia, as shown in the previously mentioned excerpt from *Hamlet* (Shakespeare, 2007). This is because in his opinion, "when Hamlet orders Ophelia 'Get thee to a nunnery,' he was using Elizabethan slang for 'whorehouse.'"

Nonetheless, for various reasons, many usually overlook the naughty side of the 16th century playwright, such as his using puns to sneak in questionable content, and there were many. For instance, some examples of Shakespeare's (2007) writings deemed risqué for various reasons are, "thereby hangs the tale," "by many a wind instrument that I know," *Hamlet*, Act III, Scene II; "Her boat hath a leak," *King Lear*, Act III, Scene VI; "There be her very C's, her U's, and her T's, and thus makes she her great P's," *Twelfth Night*, Act II, Scene V; "can take her cliff," *Troilus and Cressida*, Act V,

Chinese Woman, is Thy Name Frailty

Scene II; "Would they were clyster-pipes," *Othello*, Act II, Scene I.

In other words, in the quest for a Western standard and morality concerning women during the 16th century, and afterwards, the greatest English dramatist and poet leaves us on shaky grounds. This is because while most Westerners think of Shakespeare as a highbrow intellectual, many researchers, such as Mike Foster (2005), contend that the bawdy bard was a foul-mouth "horn dog" obsessed with sex, whose plays were filled with obscenity and very racy themes. In a quest for a Western standard of morality, he leaves us with little solace.

If not for the seemingly strong woman role of Desdemona in *Othello* (Shakespeare, 2007), an arguable case could be made against Shakespeare as being not only the greatest English writer, but also equally the biggest sexist. Desdemona after marrying Othello, a moor, stood up to her father, Brabantio, who protested to the marriage. Desdemona, unlike Hamlet with Ophelia and her over dependence on her father, told Brabantio that although she loved him, she would live her own life. *Othello* may even present more racist themes then sexism. For instance, Iago tells Brabantio, "an old black ram is tupping your white ewe" and refers to Othello as a "blacker devil." Iago also warns Brabantio that Othello and his daughter are "making the beast with two backs" (Shakespeare, 2007, in *Othello*, Act I, Scene I).

There is also the biblical expression for the origin of man and woman, and arguably an original value for womanhood. There is perhaps no better representation of Western culture, moralism and womanhood than the *Bible* (Carroll and Prickett, 2008), especially Euro-Christianity. Relevant portions of the *Bible* (King James Version Bible, Genesis: 1:23-

27, 2:2, 2:8, 2:18, 2:21-24), in particular, the Book of Genesis, read as follows.

> And the evening and the morning were the fifth day… And God said, Let us make man in our image, after our likeness: and let them have dominion over the fish of the sea, and over the fowl of the air, and over the cattle, and over all the earth, and over every creeping thing that creepeth upon the earth… So God created man in his own image, in the image of God created he him; male and female created he them… And on the seventh day God ended his work which he had made; and he rested on the seventh day from all his work which he had made… And the LORD God planted a garden eastward in Eden; and there he put the man whom he had formed…And the LORD God said, It is not good that the man should be alone; I will make him an help meet for him… And the LORD God caused a deep sleep to fall upon Adam, and he slept: and he took one of his ribs, and closed up the flesh instead thereof;… And the rib, which the LORD God had taken from man, made he a woman, and brought her unto the man… And Adam said, This is now bone of my bones, and flesh of my flesh: she shall be called Woman, because she was taken out of Man… Therefore shall a man leave his father and his mother, and

> shall cleave unto his wife: and they shall be
> one flesh.

From the *Bible* (Carroll and Prickett, 2008), it seems reasonable to surmise that Eve was a part of Adam, being one of his ribs, and Adam treated Eve as if she was a part of himself. The *Bible* at least pronounces Adam and Eve as having come either directly or indirectly from the same source. The latter does not resolve the problem of social inequality between men and women in Western societies, however.

In Western society and culture, the Book of Genesis and the creation of Adam and Eve became a controversial subject of sexism. There are diverging viewpoints, however, because in the context of Western culture and sexism, some sources would characterize the Book of Genesis and the creation of woman as the beginning of sexism. Other sources simply consider the story of creation as clearly outlining woman's inferior position to man.

There are also opposing viewpoints proclaiming that God created men and women as social equals. No doubt, these viewpoints stem from so-called moderate Christians, who may be willing to open the pulpits and priesthoods to women followers. Notwithstanding issues such as irreconcilable interpretations of what it means to be a Christian in Western society, the problem of Genesis, creation, man and woman, and especially sexism, flows from Western tradition, culture, and even systemic organizational issues.

In ancient Israel, as one source observed, they perceived women as a commodity, while Greco-Roman culture regales them to the domestic. Once early Christianity allowed woman to participate in public life, after earlier being relegated to the domestic, a medieval world embraces a religious dogma that places women at the bottom of the social hierarchy. As for the Renaissance, the supposed pillar of increasing tolerance, the Reformation placed more emphasis on married woman. In modern times, admittedly, women did eventually become active in humanitarian causes, which would enable them to draw parallels to their own plight, while also gradually demanding greater social equality (Kvam, Schearing, and Ziegler, 1998).

Another source, Elizabeth Cady Stanton (1896), also earlier wrote, "The Bible and Church have been the greatest stumbling blocks in the way of women's emancipation . . . The whole tone of Church teaching in regard to women is, to the last degree, contemptuous and degrading . . . The religious superstitions of women perpetuate their bondage more than all other adverse influences."

A problem for many societies is that true social equality between men and women has sadly become dependent on laws made by politicians and religious dogma. Moreover, it leaves Western society with a questionable standard and morality concerning womanhood. In terms of judging the state of womanhood in China, it arguably leaves us without a meaningful model for measurement. In this respect, as we explore the state of womanhood in China, Westerners and other non-Chinese people should not judge harshly.

As previously mentioned, Shakespeare (2007), in *Hamlet*, Act 1, Scene 2, wrote, "Frailty, thy name is woman." The latter begs the question, Chinese woman what is your name? Her name will be found in the history of China, both ancient and modern, as well as in Chinese classical novels, songs, poems, art, and literature, including modern art and other modern forms of expression.

5

Her Spirit Demoralized

Confucianism focuses on the criterion of fiduciary duties and responsibilities of individuals in the family and society, or social relations. The purpose of these traditional criterions is sustaining order in both the family and society. In terms of the typical relationship between a man and woman, this meant that marriage was not a love feast; rather it becomes the business of the procreation of children within the family network (or family clan) and continuing the family network, or family clan.

In traditional culture, woman, the wife, was the female form of her husband, the master of the family. The duty of a wife was to preserve the harmony of the family, which she did so by setting a moral example for the family. A love, if any, birthed from this unique relationship bound in tradition eventually produced a rigidity and lack of mutual-attraction between wife and husband. The lack of mutual-attraction, perhaps genuine love between a wife and husband, often resulted in a concubine assuming, in part, the duties of a wife. For instance, Yan Jinfen (2002) observes that, according to the acceptable practices of concubinage and polygamy, a concubine as an instrument could fulfill a husband's desire, and sometimes continue the family clan, if the wife did not produce a son (i.e., *buxiao you shan, wu hou wei da*).

The *Liji* or *Book of Rites* is a collection of ritual matters written during the late Warring States (5th cent.-221 BCE) and Former Han (206 BCE-8 CE) periods (Legge, 1967) In the *Book of Rites*, there is the section titled, "Hunyi – The Meaning of the Marriage Ceremony." In the *Liji's Hunyi*, the meaning of marriage is essentially definable as the greater good (*summun bonum*) of man and woman. Feng Yu-lan (1991) attributes this ideal based on marriage as being a duty to worship the temple of the clan and sustain the family tree. All of which constitutes filial piety (*xiao shun*), or at least a part of the concept of filial piety. This is because while filial piety means taking care of loved ones such as parents, it is a much more comprehensive concept.

According to the *Classics of Filial Piety* (*Xiao Jing*, composed between 350 and 200 B.C.), there is "perfect virtue and essential principle, with which the ancient kings made the world peaceful, and the people in harmony with one another." However, and more importantly, "this perfect virtue is hsaio [*xiao shun*], and this essential principle is also hsaio [*xiao shun*]." (Barnhart, 1996; Fung, 1991).

As described by Fung Yu-lan (1991), "In the Book XIV of the *Lu-shih Chun-chui*, which is a work of that century and a product of the eclectic school, it is said: "If there is one principle by holding which one can possess all the virtues and avoid all the evils, and have a following of the whole world, it is filial piety.""

Her Spirit Demoralized

Moreover, in terms of understanding the greater comprehension of the word *hsiao* in terms of the limits of the English language term of "filial piety," Li Chi wrote, "To prepare fragrant flesh and grain which one has cooked, tasting and then presenting before one's parents, is not filial piety; it is only nourishing them" (Fung, 1991). However, many consider the latter to be an overstatement.

Under these traditional guidelines, the worst act of being non-filial is failing to birth a son (*buxiao you shan, wu hou wei da*). In traditional culture (primarily traditional Confucianism), there is no room for love between a man and woman. For women, the emphasis is on her duties of being a mother and wife. She is a good woman and is referred to as a *xian qi liang mu* (virtuous woman and good mother). It is a guideline for womanhood that persists in modern China, as men still follow this guide in looking for a "virtuous woman and good mother" in the selection of their wives.

For the modern Chinese woman, she finds the guidelines from traditional culture no less binding, because, although perhaps even unconsciously, she still strives to meet this man-set standard from Chinese antiquity of the "virtuous woman and good mother." Many still need the great praise of being the "virtuous woman and good mother." In 1942, Zhou Enlai, in his book entitled, *About Xian Qi Liang Mu and Duty of Mother (Lun Xianqi Liang Mu Yu Mu Zhi)*, earlier made a similar critique of this ideal from antiquity. He observed that so long as these old titles for women and mothers are used, we would all sink in patriarchy. How great his words are!

The concept of *xian qi liang mu* is actually an anti-thesis to the spirit of woman, both women in antiquity and modernity. The Chinese woman in both antiquity and modernity was an individual, although denied the right to pursue individualism. The ancients words embodied in the records of antiquity, as recorded by the men of the middle-age period hinted of sexism, while clearly delineating a social hierarchy for man and woman, which manifested social inequality between man and woman.

Man-made rules would set the standard of moralism and sexism, which was to the exclusion of concerns for womanhood. Problematic is a modern Chinese culture where traditional Chinese culture (primarily traditional Confucianism) is persistent and systemic. As previously mentioned, in modern China many women amazingly still strive for this man-set higher standard of the "virtuous woman and good mother." Although the words of "virtuous woman and good mother" are innocuous in and of themselves, it is the dangerous hints or unobserved meanings that continue to subjugate modern women to second-class citizenship, let only social inequality between men and women.

In their hearts, they long for greater independence and equality, but in their minds, they feel it is only a fleeting thought. They want independence, and all other matters that make for a full, lively, and more colorful life. More importantly, those realizing the true state of social inequality between men and women, want to set to their own standards for moralism, or at least participate with men in the process of setting the standards and morals for China, especially concerning social equality between men and women.

Then there are the nuances of the language of Chinese culture. For instance, Chinese characters are probably the most difficult of all characters to learn and understand. Victor H. Mair (2002) described the Chinese system of writing as dating back to the Yellow Emperor. "Tracing them back to the time of the Yellow Emperor, Cang Jie created characters as pictographs, indicatives, associative compounds, figurative extensions, pictophonograms, and phonetic loans."

For the woman, the form of the character that employs to describe her would be the word (or character) of "*nv*." A problem is that the pictograph or pictophonogram of *nv* is a person kneeling. Quoting Qing Mu, Confucius said, "Only the woman and the small person are difficult to deal with." In addition, "if you get to close to them, they think you offend them." "If you stay far away from them, they blame you" (Fung, 1991).

The latter sentence seems to be correct concerning man. This is because men in earlier times thought you could not treat woman in a right way or perhaps a decent way. These sentences show little appreciation for women, perhaps looking down on them. In modern society, this is perhaps still true in Chinese culture. What led Confucius to look down on women and make such comments concerning them derives, at least in part, from the practice or principle of male dominance, or perhaps even sexism in antiquity.

As the close of the Qing Dynasty approached, China would commence changes that would seem to take into consideration the plight of the Chinese woman. Jiang Jinsong (2002) observes that in the aftermath of the Sino-British Opium Wars (1839-1842 and 1856-1860), forces for modernization resulted in a shift from dynastic government to constitutional government, and eventually culminated in the 1911 fall of the Qing Dynasty. There were three period of transition. More importantly, an entrepreneurial class urging a constitutional monarchy, namely, Kang Youwei, Liang Qichao, and Yan Fu, led the second period, during the 1890s.

Two historical figures, in particular, Kang Youwei and Liang Qichao seemed to lead in what appeared to be a rising women's rights movement. In an argument resembling a Chinese Renaissance during the transition from Ming Dynasty to Qing Dynasty, Wong Yin Lee (1975) translated Kang's seeming advocacy for sexual equality as follows.

> People of the world, do you wish to eliminate the evils of private ownership? To eliminate the conflicts between countries and to rid nations of border disputes? People of the world, do you wish to give peace a chance and live in a united world of harmony? The answer lies in the independence of individuals and the equality of both sexes! And these are our God-given rights.

Liang offered Chinese traditional culture new dimensions for defining what constituted a "virtuous wife and good mother." His dimensions and vision for sexual equality would still be a limited one, however. This is because from Liang's perspective, an educated girl rather than uneducated girl would be better equipped for her duties as a wife and mother. Liang may have been over-emphasizing the inadequacies of the practice of bringing girls up at home, as his solution would be a separate school for young girls, which is still sexual inequality. As previously mentioned, Liang was fostering the education of girls to allow them to be better wives for their husband. Nonetheless, given the period and turmoil during the turn of the 19th century, his ideas were revolutionary, especially a school for girls.

As Wong Lin Lee (1995) observed, "It was only after the Sino-Japanese War (1894-1895) at the end of the Qing Dynasty that a campaign to establish girls's schools began in China. At the same time changes started to take place in women's education, heralding the beginning of sexual equality within education." Further, he wrote, "Prior to the end of the Qing Dynasty (1644-1911), women's education was different, not only from that today but also from that of men at that time. The aim of traditional women's education was limited to teaching of social ethics and family traditions with an emphasis on how to become a virtuous wife and good mother."

The Qing Dynasty did fall during the Chinese Revolution of 1911, and there was a movement towards her greater liberalization. For instance, although a seemingly simplistic notion, women or woman would soon become, "her." In the Chinese of language of *Putonghua* (Mandarin), the word (or character) for "her" is *ta*. It is generally recognized that the concept of a word (or character) associated with "her" did not exist until the 1920s. The first known instance of *ta*, being using in Chinese literature is in modern Chinese literature. It is from a poem penned by Liu Bang Nong (or Liu Fu). Liu Bang Nong is the pen name of Liu Fu. He wrote a famous love poem entitled, *Jiao Wo Ruhe Bu Xiang Ta* ("Help me to know how I cannot think of her," 1926).

In *Pinyin*, this poem reads: *Jiao wo ruhe bu xiang ta: tian shang piao zhuo xie weiyun, di shang chui zhuo xie weifeng, a, weifeng chuidong le wo toufa, jia wo ruhe bu xiang ta; yueguang lian ai zhuo haiyang, haiying lian ai zhuo yueguan, a, zhe ban mi shi de yinye, jiao wo ruhe bu xiang ta; shuimian luohua manman liu, shuidi yv er manman you, a, yanzi ni shuo xie shenme hua, jiao wo ruhe bu xiang ta; kushu zai lengfeng li yao, yehuo zai muse zhong shao, a, xitian hai you xie chan xia, jiao wo ruhe bu xiang ta.*[2]

An English translation reads as follows.

_____

[2] Author's *Pinyin* translation.

Eggs under a Red Flag

Light clouds float across sky
Light winds blow on earth
Ah
Light wind touches my hair
Help me to know how I cannot think of her

Moon light loves the ocean
Ocean loves the moon
Ah
Night light is sticky like honey
Help me to know how I cannot think of her

Fallen flowers drift on water
Fish swimming slowly in water
Ah
Swallow bird what are you going to say
Help me to know how I cannot think of her

Sere trees rock in chilly winds
Wild fires burn in twilights
Ah
Sunset glow lingers in the west
Help me to know how I cannot think of her.

Liu Fu (pen name, Liu Bang Nong) was a part of the generation of innovative writers and artists during the 1920s and 1930s, who have been associated with what has been termed a then new Chinese Renaissance (*Zhongguo De Wenyi Fuxing*), which also reflected the new Cultural Movement. As an outgrowth of the May Fourth Movement, as Hu Shi (1934) explained, "[B]eginning in 1915, a strong intellectual movement was well under way, known as the New Culture Movement." Some of the members of this distinct literary gathering were Lu Xun, Hu Shi, Li Jinxi, Lin Yutang, Zhao Yuanren, and Qian Xuantong.

In 1917, the American-educated scholar Hu Shi may have proposed a major new direction for Chinese literature and language, but it is Lu Xun, who most generally regard as China's Shakespeare or the greatest Chinese writer of the 20th century. Lu Xun was adamant about changing the Chinese writing system and script, and was reportedly proclaiming that before his death, *Hanzi bu mie, Zhongguo bi wang* (If Chinese characters do not fade away, China will perish!).

During this period, as Tang Tao (1993) also recognized, Lu Xun was resolute and completely positive in his support for the revolutionary literature and the proletarian literature. Lu Xun, in his article, "*Wenyi yu geming*" ("Literature, Art and Revolution"), also wrote, "Revolution often breaks out in the world. Naturally, there will be revolutionary literature. Some of the people have woken up ... Naturally, there will be literature of the people. To put it plainly, it is the literature of another class, the fourth class" (Tang, 1993; Lu, 1991).

Additionally, it is Lu Xun's *Kuangren riji* ("The Diary of a Madman," 1918), which is considered the first text of Chinese modernity. The new movement called for using China's vernacular language (*bai hua*) as the written language. Lu Xun's famous "Diary of a Madman" was actually the first short story written in the vernacular language. The influence of Western culture was obvious, because during the Western Renaissance it was Dante Alighieri, in *De vulgari eloquentia* (c1305) (*On Eloquence in the Vernacular*), who shocked a Western world by writing in the vernacular language of Italian.

Eggs under a Red Flag

What follows in 1919 is the adoption of the vernacular language of Beijing as the national language (*guo yu*). The focus of this gathering of writers also took a sharp turn on May 4, 1919, which characterizes an attack on traditional Confucianism and Western ideals. Following the May 4, 1919 Movement (*Wu shi yundong*), their works turned toward critical realism with a strong social commentary. Although some supported *art-for-art's-sake*, the momentum turned toward *art-for-society's sake*, with critical realism at the helm until the 1940s. In the waning hours of critical realism (i.e., 1940s), a prime example of this art form or *art-for-society's* sake is arguably Ch'ien Chung-shu's novel, *Wei Cheng* (*Fortress Besieged*, 1946), which is given more attention in Chapter Seven.

However, it is Liu Fu (or Liu Bang Nong), who is generally said to be responsible for the revolutionary concept of *ta*. This is because it is the first time the cultural mainstream has addressed a new view towards the relationship between man and woman. This is the realization of the notion regarding social equality between men and women. Typical of the period was the slogan, *Ren de fa xian*, essentially meaning find the human "being," and, in turn, find woman.

At the turn of the 19th century, Chinese scholars would find themselves caught in a struggle to define the individual, if not individualism. It was a problem of defining the existence, or non-existence, of a distinctive ontology (or the science of being) in traditional China, which would translate into a meaningful concept of "Being" in modern China. For instance, can "Being" be translated unequivocally into one Chinese word (or characters), or is it a word (or characters) with many meanings equivalent to several different Chinese words (or characters)? If it, or "Being," constitutes a word (or characters) with different meanings associated with different Chinese words (or characters), then "which one is correlated to 'being'?" In particular, can "Being" be correlated to "Existence is" (*cunzai*); "is-ness" (*shi*); or "having" (*you*)? (Killion, 2006; Zhang, 2005; Zhao, 2005).

Moreover, both the new Chinese Renaissance and new Cultural Movement would parallel an earlier Western Renaissance (*Rinascimento*) of the 16th century that marked a turning point for Western civilization. The new Chinese Renaissance was not the first Renaissance in Chinese history, because during the 16th century, China witnesses a similar period of enlightenment. During the transition from the Ming Dynasty to the Qing Dynasty, there emerged an earlier and new intellectual awakening of humanity and humanism, and in the sphere of political thought, it manifested itself in the formation of democratic ideas with a distinctive modern hue.

Conversely, some Chinese sources have described this second Chinese Renaissance Movement more so in terms of Chinese Romanticism. According to this viewpoint, the innovative literature produced during this period, which followed the May Fourth Movement, is more rightly describable as a Chinese Romanticism Movement, rather than a Chinese Renaissance. Some Chinese sources characterized the lives and works of several of these writers to be representative of the development of a "new type of May Fourth personality," rather than a Renaissance in pursuit of a greater degree of humanism in Chinese society.

These Chinese sources characterized writers such as Lin Shu and Su Manshu, as belonging to a late Qing and early Republican precursors of the Romantics of the 1920s. Further, many describe Yu Dafu and Zu Zhimo as representative of that generation, and Guo Moruo, Jiang

Guangci and Xiao Jun as demonstrating the transition to what was termed revolutionary Romanticism.

Additionally, many simply characterized this period as one of Romanticism reflecting sentimentalism and dynamism. In this respect, the May Fourth generation was merely relegated to an emotional subjective strand of late Qing literature, which was subsequently pursued by the influence (or "butterly fiction") of treaty port newspapers. All of which, supposedly, enhanced the receptivity of the May Fourth generation to the sentimentalism of 19th century Western fiction, in particular, European literature.

For these reasons, the dynamics of Western culture suffers minimization, because the activities of this generation characterize an innovation that did not have a counterpart in the late Qing. As observed by Leo Ou-fan Lee (1973), in this respect, this effectually reduces the second Chinese Renaissance to the activities of a gathering of intellectuals aspiring to revitalize a culture seemingly drained of regenerative potentials. The concerns for greater humanism and democratic liberty are dismissed as seemingly unimportant, as equally seeming true for social equality for women.

Finally, the new Chinese Renaissance and new Culture Movement came to an end by the 1940s, and arguably so did many hopes for social equality between men and women. The problems of women, especially the pursuit of equality and greater independence, would once again turn to the dangerous hints or unobserved meanings that continue to subjugate modern women to second-class citizenship, let alone social inequality between men and women.

6

Ghosts, Vixens,
and "Fox Spirits"

In early China, one finds an intermixing or the meshing together of Chinese traditional culture, the social culture, social behavior, and the social system. For instance, the *Yi*, or *Yi Jing*, or the *I Ching* (*Book of Changes*), also addresses the relationship between man and woman, and the social inequality between them.

According to the *Book of Changes*, as concerns man and woman, *Qian dao cheng nan, kun dao cheng nv, bi hu wei zi qian, ke hu wei zi kun, qian jian ye, kun shun ye, qian tian ye, gu cheng wei fu, kun di ye gu cheng wei mu*. In explanation of the latter dualities, *Qian* means heaven, *kun* means earth, *qiankun* means male and female, *qian* also means open doors, *kun* also means close doors, being *qian* is strong, being *kun* is soft, *qian* is the heaven and father, and *kun* is the earth and mother.[3] In this excerpt taken from the *Book of Changes*, it is important to observe that there are dualities that lend to interpretations, perhaps even multiple interpretations and meanings.

As earlier mentioned in Chapter One, when compared to Western philosophy, Chinese art, paintings, drawings, poetry, and other arts were all full of hints, requiring the trained eye to extrapolate from generalities the specific meanings. "When one begins to read Chinese philosophical works, the first impression one gets is perhaps the briefness and disconnectedness of the sayings and writings of their authors. Open the Analects of Confucius and you will see that each paragraph consists of only a few words, and there is hardly any connection between one paragraph and the next" (Fung, 1991). It is perhaps the hints or unobserved meanings that one must discover.

In one of the simplest, clearest, and most straightforward dualities, the *Yi Jing* essentially says that man is the sky and woman is the earth. More accurately, the duality reads as follows.

> The ancients said that the relationship between the wife and her husband was like that of the minister and his ruler, and so men took precedence over women and men were honorable while women were contemptible. From this every evil theory designed to keep women from having freedom followed . . . . Men were to heaven as women were to earth and men were yang while women were yin. An absolute inequal-

---

[3] Author's *Pinyin* translation.

ity has accordingly formed between men
and women. Alas! (DeBray, 1998; Eaton,
1998).

In terms of the *yinyang* conceptualization, *yin* originally meant the absence of sunshine, therefore representing the darker and more passive elements, whereas, *yang* originally meant sunshine, which are the brighter and more active elements. In terms of what many deem Chinese philosophy, according to Vitaly A. Rubin (1982), it is a pairing dating back to the Confucian School in early Chinese antiquity, and is prominent in the teachings of Taoism.

Accordingly, the heaven covered the earth, and brings sunshine and rain to the earth. The earth arguably stands against heaven, because heaven gives and the earth takes, as in a benefactor-beneficiary relationship between man and woman. Man gives and woman takes, thus leaving the beneficiary-woman with the sole recourse of thanking her benefactor-man.

Additionally, in China, the dragon symbolizes man, whereas, the phoenix symbolizes woman. From Chinese antiquity, early artistic drawings show the dragon on top, while the phoenix typically situates in the lower portion of these drawings. During the Qing Dynasty, this cultural phenomenon would face a challenge, however.

This is because it was during the Qing Dynasty, the last dynasty of China, that Chi Xi, a woman, although not an empress, held the same the power as that of an emperor (or ruler), by virtue of her nephew sitting on the throne. It was power that historically belongs to men. It is only during this period in Chinese dynastic history that artistic drawings depicted the dragon in the lower portion of the drawing, with the phoenix now in the upper portion. In Chinese dynastic history, this is the only artistic form of expression challenging a male dominated society.

There is another exception to the ruler normally being a man, however. This is because in early Chinese dynastic history, during the Tang Dynasty, one woman did ascend to the throne, or empress, she was Empress Wu Zetian (625-705). History, records, and artistic forms of expression, however, were not very kind to her reign as empress. Perhaps because of a male dominated society being set against her, the records show that she ruled with a degree of ruthlessness.

According to the records, Empress Wu had her own son put to death, as well as large numbers of citizens. Many scholars and historians still characterize her as one of the most ruthless rulers in dynastic history, which may be due to male scholars, historians, and writers recording early dynastic history. Her rule also did not challenge a male dominated society, especially when compared to what later would occur during period of Chi Xi.

There has specifically been a moralism for women, and the measure of morality for women has traditionally been that of women with knowledge versus the desire that women have "no" knowledge. The ideal and moral woman would be a woman who had "no" knowledge, and as a direct consequence, there is the denial of learning for women. There were only a few exceptions to this general rule. In Chinese culture and history, men generally monopolized any real power, such as power in governance, power in literature, power in arts, and any other meaningful power in society. In early China, men would also set and determine life, values, and morals.

Then there is the Chinese classic of mythical literature written by Xu Zhonglin, which is the classic novel of *Feng-*

Ghosts, Vixens, and "Fox Spirits"

sheng Yanyi (*Creation of the Gods*) (Gu, 1992). The novel was written during the Yuan Dynasty, but published in the Ming Dynasty (1368-1644). The novel, *Creation of the Gods*, shows the plight of those deemed a scarlet woman, and arguably, how the standards of life, values, and morals evolved. It is a fictional tale set during the pre-Qin confederation period of the Shang (BC 1700-1050). From a mythological perspective, *Creation of the Gods* presents an account of the fall of the last emperor of the Shang (1700 BC to 1100 BC) and birth of the Zhou (1066 BC – 256 BC). This novel, like many Chinese novels, survived the generations as a folk tale from Chinese antiquity.

Many deem the *Shiji* (*Records of the Grand Historian* or *The Historical Records*, written from 109 BC to 91 BC) as the magnum opus of Sima Qian. According to the *Records of the Grand Historian* (Sima, 2007), which details the story of King Zhou and Daji, *Creation of the Gods* did not appear in book form until the Ming Dynasty (1368-1644). It would later appear, during the Qing Dynasty (1644-1911), as block-print editions.

The story concerns King Zhou, who many repute as being one of the most notorious tyrants in ancient history. He was cruel, lascivious, and generally thought to be one of the worst of all rulers. In this tale of ancient China, Zhou became overwhelmed with the beauty of a concubine named Daji. Her father, Su Hu, had sent Daji to the palace, lest she and every member of their family would suffer the penalty of death, because of earlier insults to King Zhou.

First, Su Hu insulted Zhou by not heeding his request to have Daji serve him in the rear palace. Zhou had heard that Daji was mild, virtuous, and modest. In denial of the king's wish, Su Hu retorted, "Your Majesty's got a queen consort and thousands of concubines. They're all charming and beautiful and possess talents to please all of your senses. How is it that you are so unwise as to be deluded by your lying courtiers?"

Second, there is the explosive poem written by Su Hu that offended King Zhou, which reads as follows.

> You ignore the rites between king and ministers,
> You corrupt the five cardinal virtues of manking.
> Thus, Su Hu, the Marquis of Jizhou, had decided
> to offer no further obeisance to the Shang Dynasty.

After Daji entered the palace, King Zhou ordered the West Grand Duke to punish Su Hu for offending him. The West Grand Duke, instead of punishing Su Hu, wrote a letter to Su Hu. First, the letter set forth the advantages to Su Hu of sending his daughter, Daji, to the royal palace. Second, the same letter set forth "three terrible things" that will happen if Su Hu failed to do so. Su Hu eventually agreed to send his daughter to the palace, but doing so under duress. He found himself faced with the choice of death by decapitation for treacherous acts versus a pardon.

Zhou's first sight of Daji follows.

> King Zhou fixed his eyes on her, She has soft black hair, cheeks as pretty as peach blossoms, a body slender as a tender willow branch, and was dressed as elegantly a floating clouds. She gave one the impression of a begonia drunk with sunshine, or a pear blossom drenched in rain. She was as ethereal as a fairy from either the Ninth Heaven, or the moon palace. When she partly her cherry lips, she gave off a breath of per-

> fumed fragrance. Her eyes were like autumn
> ripples, radiating coquettish charm.

To say that Zhou was pleased is an understatement; he "was entirely bewitched and seemed to be flying towards the sky." Daji would eventual ascend to the title of Queen Daji.

In this classic novel, she is also described as, "beautiful, radiating as much sweetness and charm as peony blossoms dripping with dew." She was so beautiful that she captured the king's eye, and he found himself at a loss because of her beauty. For pleasing this beauty, the king found himself committing foolish acts, as "he continued to indulge with Daji day and night, ignoring all state affairs." Zhao Qi cries out at the king, "You wretched tyrant! You've killed your prime minister, forsaken the loyal and gravely disappointed your dukes. You trust in Daji, listen to the minions and propel the state towards ruin."

The king's folly eventually resulted in the king killing both the state and himself. The irony of this story is that Chinese literature interpreted King Zhou as having found himself deceived (or deluded) by the beautiful concubine named Daji, because of her beauty. In the literature of Chinese antiquity, the problem was not attributable to King Zhou himself. Rather, the cause of King Zhou's problems had been Daji. In addition, the problem of Daji stemmed from the added problem that many would describe as a "fox spirit" (*huli jing*). As the classic tale reads,

> What Su Hu did not know that the woman
> whom he talked to was none other than the
> thousand-year-old fox sprite [spirit]. During
> the few minutes it took him to return to his
> room for a second lamp, the fox sprite

[spirit] had sucked out Daji's soul and then occupied her body. Her purpose was to seduce King Zhou and overthrow the Shang Dynasty, as Goddess Nu Was had ordered.

For having lost a kingdom and burning himself to death, Zhou would not be blameworthy. Rather, all faults were attributable to the thousand-year-old "fox spirit."

In modern China, including modern Chinese literature, there is still reference to a so-called bad woman, scarlet woman, vulgar woman or promiscuous woman, as being a "fox spirit." For instance, in modern China one can still witness a concerned wife using the term "fox spirit," as she questions the suspect infidelity of a husband. She does so by asking her husband, who is your "fox spirit?"

Moreover, King Zhou's eventual setting himself afire as a means of death is *yin huo shao shen* (draw fire against oneself), a phrasing that one can still hear in modern China. For example, in everyday conversation, one can be heard to say that a person that did something wrong had drawn fire upon himself or herself. The person doing a wrong or misdeed, like King Zhou, assumedly, deserves a death by fire for his wrongs, because he is ultimately blameworthy for his own misdeeds.

There are also other similar fictional stories resembling the tale of Daji. For instance, during the Tang Dynasty, there is the story of Emperor Rong Ji, who encounters the beauty of Yang Yu Huan. So enamored was the Emperor by her beauty that he did not rule well, and Yang Yu Huan eventually became the scapegoat of his folly and failings. The tragedy of this story is that in the end she suffers death by hanging.

Ghosts, Vixens, and "Fox Spirits"

There is also the classic novel of Pu Songling (1640-1715), being *Liao Zhai Zhi Yi* (i.e., English translations: *Strange Stories from a Chinese Studio* or *Fairy Ghost Vixen*), which is a collection of fictional stories comprising four hundred and thirty-one stories about ghosts, fairies, and "fox spirits" (Pu, 1880). *Liao Zhai Zhi Yi* was written during the late Ming Dynasty and early Qing Dynasty.

As for stories such as *Liao Zhai Zhi Yi* and others of this period, they may have been either good or bad for the movement toward greater humanism, being the new and first Chinese Renaissance. In this respect, good in the sense that these stories may have challenged a society bound by conventionalism or traditional Chinese culture, and arguably sought to enlighten the people. The problem is whether they could be said to be an attempt to enlighten men, or both men and women. This is because these stories more likely than not frustrated the movement towards greater humanism with these dream-like visions of men. Leaving us to wonder just who was going to be enlightened, and what sort of enlightenment that was especially sought by the men of scholarship, art, and literature.

Nonetheless, the book contains romantic words, when creating beautiful ghosts, by using dream-like words. Although in *Liao Zhai Zhi Yi*, there is a description of what seems to be a different "fox spirit," it remains the same "fox spirit" seen or read about in other novels or sources. It is a description that is vivid with striking colors, while also vividly describing both the fear of men and lure of the "fox spirit," but still similar to that described by others because all "fox spirits" are beautiful women.

The moral of these stories are all the same. There are many similar stories in the history of China owing to the beauty of a woman. In Chinese antiquity, the beauty of a woman also associates with a beautiful women potentially being a *huo shui* (troublemaker). When a man consumed her beauty, then troubles were thought to flow to the man. When the troubles of a man coincided with the admirations of a beautiful woman, then ensuing trouble was always the fault of the scapegoat woman, who would normally be the ghost, vixen, or "fox spirit".

The man himself, so troubled, also did not think troubles attributable to his own personal acts. It was the fault of the *huo shui*, and not the man. The irony of this travesty is that not only did the consuming man and the other men agree on this idea, the women also agreed they were blameworthy. In this respect, the actions of women in general were arguably tantamount to a sort of collective and intellectual suicide.

As previously mentioned, stories similar to the story of Daji are found not only in this novel, but also in other sources. In the classical Chinese works, one can find the same "trouble makers" and "fox spirits." From the *Xi Han Chao* (Western Han Dynasty), there is also the classic of *Lie Nv Zhuan* (i.e., English translations: *Collection of Woman Stories* or *Biographies of Exemplary Women*), which was written by the Han Dynasty scholar Liu Xiang. The classic of *Lie Nv Zhuan* is distinguishable as the first book to focus on a collection of studies concerning women (Lin, 2005). The novel *Lie Nv Zhuan*, like another classical novel, *Nv Xun*, also distinguishably served as instructions to women on how to comply with the man-made rules of an indifferent feudal society.

The *Collection of Woman Stories* contains one hundred and five stories and, in this volume, one can also find the fictional story of "Mei Xi," a beautiful woman of the late Xia, which is a pre-Qing Dynasty confederation. There is also contained in the *Collection of Woman Stories*, the fictional story

Ghosts, Vixens, and "Fox Spirits"

of "Bao Yi," of the late *Xi Zhou* (Western Zhou), another pre-Qing Dynasty confederation). There is also the non-fictional story of "Cheng Yuan Yuan" of the late Ming Dynasty.

Moreover, the scholars, artists, and writers of the Middle Ages greatly contributed to both the development of Chinese culture and ideals concerning woman, such as the concepts of *huo shui*, *huli jing*, and other ideas casting women in an unfavorable light. The same is true in modern times. In modern China, one need only turn to the life of Jiang Qian for a modern day example of the classic story of the beautiful Chinese woman turned "trouble maker" (*huo shui*). The life of Jiang Qian, the third wife of Mao Zedong (Tsetung) (1893–1976), also arguably demonstrates the previously mentioned concept of the "fox spirit." In modern Chinese society, her story illustrates this continuing unique conceptualization of women.

When Jiang Qian met Mao Zedong, she was of the age of 26, and he was of the age of 42. He was also a deity-like figure in China, the most powerful man in China. When Mao lectured to students, Jiang Qian, the young student, always managed to find a seat in the first row of seats. He captivated her. From a woman's point of view, her falling in love with Chairman Mao made sense. Perhaps the relationship between Jiang Qian and Mao was no different from that between any other man and woman.

In the public eye, people still generally believe that, at least in part, it was because of Jiang Qian that Mao made the mistake of starting the Great Cultural Revolution (*Wenhua Da Geming*) (1966-1976), including the mistakes made during the Great Cultural Revolution. For the Chinese, she is considered the "trouble maker" (*huo shui*), or perhaps even the "fox spirit." Perhaps the latter reflects a viewpoint and attitude toward women that persists in modern society and continues to be rooted in a dark and long ago past, being Chinese antiquity.

During the earlier Yan'an period, when Jiang Qian first met Mao, she was only 26 years of age. According to John K. Emmerson (1985), Yan'an is in Shaanxi Province, China, on the Yen River. It was the end of the route for the famous long march, and Yan'an also served as the de facto capital (1936-47, 1948-9) of the Chinese Communists, who established arsenals, colleges, and a military academy there. During the days at Yan'an, she became his personal secretary.

Having observed the growth of the relationship between Jiang Qian and Mao, high-level leaders met and refused to grant her the name of "wife of Chairman Mao" (Ye, 1992). As earlier mentioned in Chapter One, the latter is yet another phenomenon of Chinese culture and the social organization. In order to form social organizations or small groups, rules of conduct are needed.

At that time, a couple wanting to marry had first to obtain permission from relevant social organizations, such as the party acting through leaders. However, Mao insisted that they compromise, and only then did they grant her the name, "wife of Chairman Mao." According to Ye Yonglie's (1993), her last written note, which she wrote on her cell bed on May 13, 1991, which was immediately before her suicide and just four hours before, reads, "Chairman, I love you. I am always your student and soldier and I am coming to see you now."

Furthermore, in Chinese antiquity, there appears to be only one female exception to a male dominated literary world of the dream worlds of ghost, vixens, and "fox spirits." The year of 1996 revealed a newly discovered Chinese classical poem entitled, *A Plaint of Lady Wang*.

Lady Wang possibly lived around the time of Zhu Xi's life (1170-1200). According to the author of the book, *Gui Dong (Chinese Mysticism)*, which put the poem titled *A Plaint of Lady Wang* on record in the text of a story, which is the Twelfth Volume of a *Zhibuzuzhai* series, *Guidong (Chinese Mysticism)*, we only know that Lady Wang's family name was Wang. The available details of her life are scant. She was a concubine that survived a murder plot of a jealous wife and eventually became a Taoist nun. As for the penned poem, Lady Wang addressed the poem to her husband and found it lying next to his pillow the following morning (Yan, 2002).

Literally, the title of the poem *Jie Boming Tan* means "a sigh of a woman for her preordained fate." Perhaps attributable to a failed attempt on her life, the poem, at a relevant part, reads.

> Tell me, father and mother,
> Why was I born?

"The struggle of Lady Wang's soul made her question her fate (*ming*), which was imparted by Heaven according to Confucian tradition." One source described *A Plaint of Lady Wang* as a woman's struggle between traditional notions of the *hun* (mind-heart/soul/spirit) and *po* (the body person). A conversation recorded in *Zuo Zhuan* informs us that as early as the sixth century B.C.E., people thought that every person possessed *hun* and *po*: in man's life, the first transformations refer to the earthly aspect of the soul (*po*). After producing *po*, that which is strong and positive refers to *hun*, which is the heavenly aspect of the soul (*hun*).

Eggs under a Red Flag

A distinctiveness of this poem lies in the phenomenon that the study of Chinese mysticism historically did not focus on the experience of women, or the writings of women, which are not included in the classics, scriptures, and canons. The poem is introspective because it describes Lady Wang's mystical experience and real life.

In her dream, there was a direct encounter with a divine being, and there are some Romantic expressions of feelings and emotions. Poets generally use Romanticism to display earnest pursuit of the ideal realm and to pose a sharp contrast with the realistic world. Imagination, passion, and enthusiasm unrestrained and completely free are features of Romanticism in Chinese poetry and prose. In Chinese history and literature, this variety of Romanticism arguably first appears as a form of poetic and literary expression as early as the *Book of Odes*.

> Oh, my void, empty soul and body," Lady Wang sighs. But whose body is it? Who cares more about the hun/soul: man or woman? What will the future concept of the soul be? (*A Plaint of Lady Wang*).

In her dream, Lady Wang consulted with the Confucian Goddess Banji, who was the foremost Chinese woman scholar during her life time (c. 49 - c. 120) and was also called Ban Zhao or Cao Dajia; a Buddhist nun; and Lishan Laomu, a female Taoist immortal described by Li Quan of the Tang dynasty, and there were others, such as the fairy Hemp lady. However, it was only with these three that she presents the question of her preordained fate. In the end, as observed by one source, "She yearns for the limited love her husband gave her and an ideal family containing only one

wife. She blames herself and wants him to understand her."
The poem at a relevant part reads:

> Everyone has the same body,
> why are their happiness and suffering so different?

It is a cry or plea "for equality and challenge to concubinage and polygamy, which could (in different social circumstances) lead to a demand for equality between men and women" (Yan, 2002). In the dream, she gives her husband the poem and then awakes, saying, "Oh, my empty body and soul!" What is more important about the poem, *A Plaint of Lady Wang*, is that it provides at least some insight into the dream world of a woman in antiquity. Having done so, it also leaves us in awe of her struggle for equality, although it is an equality mostly bound by traditional culture.

In the end, she still shows her dependence on her husband, like Ophelia in *Hamlet* (Shakespeare, 2007), and her primary concern is returning to her traditional duties. Additionally, her dream world did not comprise the ghosts, vixens, and "fox spirits" that appeared in the dream worlds of men, or similar images of ghosts, vixens, and "fox spirits" in the forms of men. Moreover, her dream was the pursuit mostly of a search for an understanding of a preordained fate, or a fate bound by an ancient social order. Indeed, whether Lady Wang's poem is cast in terms of the *hun* (mind-heart/soul/spirit) and *po* (the body person), or a struggle of her soul making her question fate (*ming*), it is introspection by Lady Wang at best.

For the Chinese people, the image of the "fox spirit" has always been a part of mostly the Chinese male psychic, which entails philosophical, psychological, and socioeconomic dimensions. There is a much deeper consequence of the male-inspired imagery of the "fox spirit."

As previously mentioned, in the classic novel of *Liao Zhai Zhi Yi*, a "fox spirit" is described as appearing in the form of a beautiful woman with striking colors. More importantly, there are the vivid descriptions of both the fear of men and the lure of the "fox spirit." A constant characteristic of the "fox spirits" in the great novels and classics is that they always appear in the forms of beautiful women. However, it is the combination of fear and her lure, and perhaps more accurately her allure that deserves greater attention.

For man, in both antiquity and modernity, it may well be the problem of reality versus a dream world or his imagination. In reality, the classics tell us man should fear the "fox spirits" and "Dajis" of the world. However, the dream world of man, and his imagination, selected to present his supposed arch nemesis, or perhaps Greek-like mythological goddess of divine retribution and vengeance in the human forms of beautiful women. For the Chinese classics, she ("the fox spirit") may well represent man and mysticism in want of a god. Moreover, while *Liao Zhai Zhi Yi* is not rightly classified as erotica, the same may not hold true for men in their dream worlds and imaginations.

In descriptions of their images of the "fox spirits," the adjectives suggest no less, because the "fox spirits" as created by the men of literary in their folk tales and classical writings, amazingly attributed to her features both feared and desired. The many adjectives describing their "Dajis" and their desires for the "fox spirits" of their dream worlds or imaginations are a certain lure, allure, erotic appeal, being a seductive siren, nymph, and perhaps even the worst of cunning nymphomaniacs.

Ghosts, Vixens, and "Fox Spirits"

In Greek mythology, such as 1 *Odyssey*, 12, the Sirens are creatures with the head of a female and the body of a bird. They lived on an island (Sirenum Scopuli; three small rocky islands) and with the irresistible charm of their song, they lured mariners to their destruction on the rocks surrounding their island. Returning from the abode of the shades, Ulysses revisited the AEaean isle and recounted to Circe his adventures, the wondrous visions, and the laws of Hell. She in return speeded his homeward voyage, instructing him particularly how to pass safely by the coast of the Sirens (Graves, 1993; Evslin, 1980).

When analyzing "the typical character of *Lie nv Zhuan* from the perspective of gender," as Lin Cunxin (2005) explained, "the male discourse may form false value through the illusion of female images subjectively." As previously mentioned, the Chinese classic novel of *Fengsheng Yanyi* (*Creation of the Gods*) reads, "Her [Daji] purpose was to seduce King Zhou and overthrow the Shang Dynasty, as Goddess Nu Was had ordered."

In terms of the ghosts, vixens, and especially "fox spirits, the philosophical, psychological, and socio-economics dimensions are obvious and relevant, because the dangerously hidden hints and unobserved meanings may have defined, and continues to define, the relationship between men and women. This is because, in society as we know it, including Chinese society and culture, the implications of social inequality, especially between men and women, will be far-reaching and guaranteed to run its deepest course.

Lady Wang, in *A Plaint for Lady Wang*, neither found, nor pursued the ghost, vixens, and "fox spirits" of the male dream worlds. One wonders how other Chinese women in antiquity, if allowed the opportunity to take pen in hand would have described these seductive vixens and "fox spirits," or even if they would have entertained the notion of creating their images in the first instance. Given the lone example of Lady Wang's *A Plaint for Lady Wang*, it is at least reasonable to surmise that she, the Chinese woman of antiquity, cried in silence for the freedom of social equality and freedom from the practices of concubinage and polygamy.

The spirit of woman in antiquity had been demoralized. However, for now, the dye has been cast, and perhaps modern man still finds himself struggling between his realities and dream worlds or imaginations. This is because they still seem to both fear and desire the seductive ghosts, vixens, and "fox spirits" of their dream worlds and imaginations.

Men may fear and desire beautiful women, or simply, fear and desire women. As arguably one of the worst creations and consequences of scholarly, artistic, and literary men, who are charged with the highest responsibility of recording history and culture, the ghosts, vixens, and "fox spirits" of their dream worlds and imaginations may well represent or symbolize an intended, though unconsciously, demoralized spirit of the modern Chinese woman.

7

Lyrics of Lost Love

This chapter continues the underlying theme of the influence of Chinese traditional culture (particularly traditional Confucianism) on modern Chinese culture. The previously discussed theme of Chapter Six, in part, is also continued. In Chapter Six, we explored the records and sources of history and culture, which have been predominantly male-inspired visions of society, culture, morality, and virtue.

The present chapter continues this theme with slight variations, however, by exploring the topic of "lost love" in both antiquity and modernity. This chapter, like earlier chapters, does so by referring to the records and sources of culture, which reflects notions of morality (or moralism) and virtue in both antiquity and modernity. This chapter is entitled, "Lyrics of Lost Love," and commences with an examination of the ideas or ideals of love in antiquity, dating from post-Zhou Chinese culture (or traditional Confucian culture).

Eggs under a Red Flag

In order to do so, a diverse range of the records of history and culture are explored. It is a diverse range stemming from the odes of the *Shijing* (*The She King, Book of Song* or *Book of Odes*) and Chinese classical literature, such as from the novel entitled, *Jin Ping Mei* (i.e., English translations: *The Plum in the Golden Vase* or *The Golden Lotus*), to 20th-century literature such as the novel, *Wei Cheng* (*Fortress Beseiged*), and others records of modern Chinese history, literature, and culture.

One of the earliest influence on post-Zhou Chinese culture, or traditional Confucianism, are the writings (or poems) contained in *Shijing*, which is the first record of poems collected. It is a collection of 305 poems from the Zhou (B.C. 1122 to B.C. 256) (Legge, 1994). The *Shijing* is one of the six classics; the others are namely, *The Book of History*, *The Book of Rites*, *The Book of Music*, *The Book of Changes*, and *The Spring and Autumn Annals*. All of which were distinguishable in their writing styles and contents.

According to James Legges (1994), "[T]here were originally 311 pieces; but of six of them there are only the titles remaining." Further, Father Lacharme calls the Book – Liber Carminum and with most English writers the ordinary designation of it has been The Book of Odes." In terms of dynastic history, it covers a periodical span from the *Xi Zhou* (Western Zhou), to the middle of the *Chun Qiu* (Spring and Autumn Period). It is a collection of poems from about a 500-year span of Chinese antiquity.

The collection was originally called *Shi* (Poems) and *Shi Sanbai* (Three Hundred Poems). During the Han Dynasty, Confucians would later name the collection, *Shijing*. The collection has also been referred to as *Maoshi* (Mao Poems), because it was by Mao Heng of the Han Dynasty that the *Shijing* was passed down to the present time. The poems collected are actually lyrics of various songs. It is a collection of songs from earlier folk songs also stemming from different places throughout China. The various songs collected are grouped into three different styles, which are *Feng* (Ballads), *Ya* (Festal Odes), and *Song* (Sacrificial Songs).[4]

The *Feng* consists of 160 poems, including those of 15 countries and areas. They are Zhounan (Zhou and the south), Shaonan, Bei, Yong, Wei, Wang, Zheng, Qi, Wei, Tang, Qin, Chen, Gui, Cao, and Bin. Most of the poems in *Feng* are folk songs from along the Yellow River. Only a few of them are works of the nobles. The *Ya* includes 105 poems, which are divided into Xiaoya (The Minor Festal Odes) and Daya (The Major Festal Odes). The poems in the *Ya* are mostly written by the nobles. The *Song* consists of 40 poems, including the sacrificial hymns and songs in the courts of Zhou, Lu, and Shang.

It is a collection of poems produced by a feudal and agrarian society. The collection contains poems written by common people and some written by nobles. The poems written by the common people demonstrate a harmonious picture of hard-working farmers, while also expressing their sense of life and feelings about feudal and agrarian life in early dynastic China, and many lyrics of love. Nobles write a few songs in the *Feng*, while the nobles basically write all of the poems in *Ya*. However, many consider the poems of the common people, rather than those of the nobles, to be richer in poetry and form.

Some Western experts would challenge the Romanticism of early classic literature, especially its use of nature as a theme. However, one Western source, actually, recognized

---

[4] The Shijing or "Book of Songs" is the earliest a poetry collection; http://www.chinavista.com/experience/shijing/b5shijing.html.

the differences and similarities, when comparing Western Romanticism to the later Tang Dynasty and Song Dynasty poets. The source writes, "The difference between Romantic and Chinese Tang/Song poets in their use of natural imagery is not that the former is subjective and the latter is objective, for although the Romantics use nature as a theme while the Chinese poets do not, they both employ natural imagery for expressing the inner world" (Cao, 1998; Abrams, 1984).

The *Shijing* is also important because it arguably represents the earliest notions of Romanticism in Chinese antiquity, history, and literature. In the English language, Romanticism is defined as, "An artistic and intellectual movement originating in Europe in the late 18th century and characterized by a heightened interest in nature, emphasis on the individual's expression of emotion and imagination, departure from the attitudes and forms of classicism, and rebellion against established social rules and conventions." It is also defined as simply, "Romantic quality or spirit in thought, expression, or action."

In the study of Chinese literature, a Chinese definition of Romanticism is similar to Western definitions, although slightly varied. For instance, in modern China, or at least a post-Qing dynasty China (post-1911), one can even find references to a poem written by Mao Zedong as being described by many as "revolutionary Romanticism."

In terms of classic Chinese literature, Romanticism is a state of ecstatic feelings and emotions. As a form of poetic and literary expression, Romanticism arguably first appeared in early Chinese history, or Chinese antiquity, in the *Shijing*. In subsequent periods, Romanticism can also be found in the poems authored by authors such as Qu Yuan, Bai Juyi, and Li Bai. In the ancient literature of China, such as the

Lyrics of Lost Love

Shijing, the poets of earlier periods used Romanticism for displaying the pursuit of an ideal realm, while intending to present a sharp contrast with a realistic world. Pursuant to Romanticism, a poet's imagination, passion and enthusiasm were released unconstrained.

Some argue that the latter features of Chinese Romanticism actually birthed a Chinese form of mysticism. For example, and notwithstanding Romanticism, or even arguably mystical Romanticism of the *Shijing*, a poem penned by, or at least traditionally attributed to Qu Yuan (340 BC – 278 BC) and entitled *Chu Ci* (Chu Songs) presents another, although later, example of early Romanticism in poetry. According to Yan Jinfen, based on an earlier translation by Livia Kohn, in *Taoist Mystical Philosophy: The Scripture of Western Ascension*, "Qu Yuan, a conscientious minister of Chu, was slandered and banished from the court. Despairing at the corruptness of the world, he drowned himself into the Milo River" (Yan, 2002; Kohn, 1991).

An English translation of the *Chu Ci* (Chu Songs) follows.

Pacing with restlessness, I yearn to get away,
Confused and close to madness, I long for the eternal.
My mind goes wild, strays off without control;
My heart melancholy, I am ever sadder.
Suddenly my spirit, off, never to come back,
My body, like a withered tree, left behind alone.
(The Far-off Journey) (Kohn, 1991; Yan, 2002).

The *Shijing* is equally important in other respects, which further demonstrates its power and potency. There are philosophical, psychological, historical, and perhaps even political dimensions to the *Shijing*. For instance, the political and philosophical significance of the poem, *Cai Ge*, is that it

75

reminds one of the great contributions of the *Shijing* in the history of China.

While filial piety (*xiao shun*) was one of the cornerstones of Confucianism or the School of Confucianism, the *Shijing* was one of the cornerstones of early Confucianism. For instance, the social philosophy of Confucius (551 BC - 479 BC), in part, revolved around the concept of *ren*, which are notions of "compassion" or "loving others." In order to cultivate and practice these concerns for others, one had to essentially deprecate himself. One did so by avoiding "artful speech" or an "ingratiating manner," which would create false impressions, while also leading to self-aggrandizement. In the end, for those whom managed to cultivate *ren* are the "simple in manner and slow of speech."

Moreover, Confucius taught that if one failed to cultivate and practice this keen sense of the well-being and interests of others, his ceremonial manners would signify nothing (Yang, 1956; Confucius and Lau, 1979, at *Lunyu* 1.3, 3.3 and 13.27). According to the *Analects*, Confucius said, "Zhou enjoyed the advantage of surveying the former two dynasties. How refined its culture was! It is the rites of Zhou that I'd like to follow." Confucius further said, "If I were placed in power, I would create another Zhou in the east" (Cai, 1994; He, 1991). It is the Romanticism of the *Shijing* that would later influence Confucius, his followers, and Confucianism.

There are also the political and economic dimensions. The significance of the *Shijing* to ancient China and subsequent periods is far-reaching, because the *Shijing* would substantially contribute to an evolution of various ideals in subsequent dynasties. For example, the periods from the Shang, to the Spring and Autumn period, witnessed the development of philosophical, political, and economic ideas.

Lyrics of Lost Love

In particular, the root of most economic ideas would stem from what was described in the *Book of Odes* (*Shijing*) as agricultural conditions in the Western Zhou (Gernet, 1996). The same is true regarding the development of philosophical, political, and economic ideas during the Warring States period, which continued to evolve in the later Qin Dynasty and subsequent dynasties to come. Nonetheless, it is the Romanticism of the *Shijing* that is seemingly timeless and enduring.

The Romanticism of the *Shijing* is reflected in the styles and focus of these early poems, especially those of the common people. The style and focus of these writers are distinguishable from the writings of the period scholars and philosophers that pursued distinctively different interests, rather than that of the hard-working farmers. The *Shijing* and its collections of poems are full of feelings about life. They are poems that are honest and simple, and yet, philosophical. The poems demonstrate a harmony of nature, if not a harmony with nature, specifically, the hard-working farmer being in harmony with nature. The *Shijing* addresses many aspects of the Zhou such as work and love, war and corvée, oppression and resistance, customs and marriage, sacrifices and feasts, astronomical phenomena and landforms, and animals and plants.

Furthermore, some of these poems have titles and some do not and this often results in the first sentences of some poems being used as a title. During translations, from Chinese to English, or other languages, many times an author will, simply, give a poem a name. "Some assume writers of the pieces," as Legge (1994) explained, "gave them their names themselves; and this may have been the case at times. –The subject of the name need rarely be referred to hereafter."

77

Eggs under a Red Flag

For this reason, many times the name of a poem is not as important as the contents of a poem. A sampling of three poems from *Shijing* follows. An example of one of these poems or odes is *Kwan ts'eu* (*Guan Jiu*), which is the first poem in Part I, Lessons from the States, in Book I, Odes of Chow and the South (Odes of Zhou and the South), and is the first poem in the *Book of Odes*. According to Legge (1994), and quoting Choo He, "He going to say that the princes of States collected such compositions among their people, and presented them to the king, who delivered them to the Board of music of classification." Further, Legge wrote, "The States are those of Chow, Shaou, P'ei, Yung, and the others, which give their names to the several Books."

The pieces in this section ar
e called *fung*, "because they owe their origin to and are descriptive of the influences produced by superiors, and the exhibition of this is again sufficient to affect men, just as things give forth sound, when moved by the wind, and their sound is again sufficient to move [other] things."

An English translation of *Guan Jiu* (Legge, 1994) follows.

> Guan-guan [Kwan-kwan] go the ospreys,
> On the islet in the river.
> The modest, retiring, virtuous, young lady:-
> For our price a good mate she.

> Here long, there short is the duckweed,
> To the left, to the right, borne about by the current.
> The modest, retiring, virtuous, young lady:-
> Waking and sleeping, he sought her.

In the language of *Putonghua* (Mandarin or *Pinyin*), the same poem reads as follows.

Lyrics of Lost Love

Guan guan zhi jiu
zai he zhi zhou
yaotiao shu nv
junzi haoqiu.

Cenci xingcai
zuoyou liuzhi
yaotiao shu nv
wumei qiuzhi
qiuzhi.[5]

Guan Jiu is a moving love song, in its lyrics of love. A young man fell in love with a young and pretty girl. He misses her during the hours he is awake and even in his dreams. However, he still cannot find the girl. Facing a running river and looking at playing birds, the girl seems like she appears before him. The tall grasses swaying in the wind remind him of the girl's lovely body. These scenes make him so blue and have such strong feelings about this girl that he wants to search her out and marry her.

The feelings of love contained in this poem are very straightforward and bold. The poem does not conceal the young man's true feeling and desires. This very simple, natural, and romantic love poem demonstrates the sensitivity of individual life, without any biases influenced by materialism or a materialistic society. *Guan Jiu* shows the freedom of being lord over the individual. Perhaps like the freedom of a bird, because a "guan jiu" is a bird.

There are also other philosophical, psychological, historical, and perhaps even political dimensions to *Guan Jiu*. As

---

[5] Author's *Pinyin* translation of *Guan Jiu*.

noted, *Guan Jiu* is produced in the translations of both an English and *Pinyin* version. A reading of the English language, when compared to the *Pinyin* translation, however, reveals that a substantial part of *Guan Jiu* was lost in translation. The English wording, although cute and still appealing, falls substantially short of the true context and meaning contained in the original *Guan Jiu*. Even assuming the English translation is correct in its interpretation of the Chinese words (or characters), it leaves much to desire.

In the original and Chinese version of the ode, as in all the others, at the end of every ode there is a given note stating first, the number of stanzas and the lines in the stanza. Second, the critical "rhymes" are set in these stanzas by an ancient indicator following a character that denotes the ancient pronunciation of it (Legge, 1994, however, "The ancient pronunciation of it, found in the odes, was different from that now belonging to it").

If a reading of *Guan Jiu* is not available in the Chinese language and speech, one cannot imagine the splendor of *Guan Jiu* when so read. It is a distinctly more moving experience, which is the distinctive sound of the Chinese pronunciations resembling the singing of a song, rather the reading of a Chinese poem translated into the English language. One source described Romantic lyrics, although from a later dynastic period, as follows.

> Some of the poems [Romantic lyrics] are called odes, while the others approach the ode in having lyric magnitude and a serious subject, feeling fully meditated. They present a determinate speaker in a particularized, and usually a localized, outdoor setting, whom we overhear as he

carries on, in a fluent vernacular which rises easily to a more formal speech, a sustained colloquy, sometimes with himself or with the outer scene, but more frequently with a silent human auditor, present or absent. The speaker begins with a description of the landscape; an aspect or change of aspect in the landscape evokes a varied but integral process of memory, thought, anticipation, and feeling which remains closely intervolved with the outer scene. In the course of this meditation, the lyric speaker achieves an insight, faces up to a tragic loss, comes to a moral decision, or resolves an emotional problem. Often the poem rounds upon itself to end where it began, at the outer scene, but with an altered mood and deepened understanding, which is the result of the intervening meditation (Abrams, 1984).

However, this is not a typical phenomenon when translating works or writings from ancient sources, or even modern Chinese works. There is always seemingly a loss of context and meanings occurring in the process of translation to another language. As previously mentioned in Chapter One, because an artist, whether writer or painter, generally intends to communicate not necessarily what is directly expressed in the artwork, but more so what is not expressed. It is especially when reading the classics of antiquity that one immediately notices the briefness and disconnectedness of the sayings and writings of their authors.

For instance, you need only, "Open the Analects of Confucius and you will see that each paragraph consists of only a few words, and there is hardly any connection between one paragraph and the next" (Fung, 1991). In traditional Chinese culture, a good poem would have "limited words (or characters), but unlimited meanings" (*yan you jing yi wu qiong*). Moreover, as perhaps a political dimension of *Guan Jiu*, it does not contain the character of *ta* (she or "her"), in reference to a woman. Rather it uses the characters *zhi* and *shu nv*.

As earlier explained in Chapter Six, it is Liu Fu (or Liu Bang Nong), who is generally said to be responsible for the revolutionary concept of *ta*. Because it is the first time, the cultural mainstream of modern China addressed a new view toward the relationship between man and woman. Liu Fu wrote the famous love poem entitled, *Jiao Wo Ruhe Bu Xiang Ta* ("Help me to know how I cannot think of her"). It is the consequence of the new Chinese Renaissance and new Cultural Movement that would parallel an earlier Western Renaissance (*Rinascimento*) of the 16th century, as expressed by the period-slogan, *Ren de fa xian*.

Since antiquity, the ode of *Guan Jiu* has also been the subject of different translations, resulting in different interpretations of the stanzas. From the schools of Maou and Chou, to James Legge, the interpretations have varied. The different interpretations are from celebrating the virtue of the bride of King Wan, a celebration of the bride or queen of Duke Zhou's (Chow) father during the later Han Dynasty, the celebration of virgin purity as a flower unseen (first stanza), friends of bridegroom expressing joy of marriage, to Legge's insistence there is no mention of King Wan and the lady "Sz" in *Guan Jiu*, and other interpretations.

A sampling of other translations and interpretations are: Yuan Zhong Xu's translation of the *Shi Jing* (1993); William Jennings's *The Shi King: The Old "Poetry Classic" of the Chinese*

Lyrics of Lost Love

(1969); Ezra Pound's *The Classic Anthology Defined by Confucius* (1954); Bernhard Karlgren's *The Book of Odes* (1950); and Yang Yixian's *The Book of Songs* (2001).

Additionally, while Confucius expressed admiration for this ode, his words of admiration were of no help in interpreting the ode (Legge, 1994). Given that the ode is in the *Feng* style, in conjunction with many interpreting odes as a celebration of love between nobility, it was arguably written by one of the nobles. All of which is another issue of interpretation, perhaps serving as an added example of the problems of interpreting these odes.

There is also a historical dimension to *Guan Jiu*. During the pre-Great Cultural Revolution period, one would find this poem being routinely taught in the classrooms of China, as the students joining in union would read the poem together in their native tongue. Oh, how splendid the sounds of the lyrics were!

For instance, during the pre-Great Cultural Revolution period, so stimulating was the *Guan Jiu* perceived to be that some mothers protested their children having to read aloud in class the lyrics of *Guan Jiu*. Indeed, *Guan Jiu* was about love, and more importantly bold love. One wonders whether the objections of these mothers were more so a concern with bold love, rather then teaching their children the possible lessons of being lord over the individual.

Another example of one of these poems or odes is *Ts'ae koh* (*Cai Ge*), which also comes form Part I, Lessons from the States, in Book VI, The Odes of Wang (The Odes of the Royal Family Doman). An English translation of *Cai Ge* (Legge, 1994) follows.

> There he is gathering the dolichos!
> A day without seeing him

Is like three months!

There he is gathering the oxtail-southern wood!
A day without seeing him
Is like three seasons!

There he is gathering the mugwort!
A day without seeing him
Is like three years!

The poem *Cai Ge* is produced as follows, as translated into the language of *Putonghua* (Mandarin or *Pinyin*).

Bi cai ge xi
Yi ri bu jian
Ru san yue xi.

Bi cai xiao xi
Yi ri bu jian
Ru san qiu xi.

Bi cia ai xi
Yi ri bu jian
Ru san yue xi.[6]

It is obvious that *Cai Ge* is a love poem. A young woman wrote it, so it is also love from a woman's point for view. There are three important lines in the stanza, "Is like three months," "Is like three season," and "Is like three years." From three months, three seasons, to three years, her affections for a young man grow strong and then stronger. In

---

[6] Author's *Pinyin* translation of *Cai Ge*.

modern China, they still borrow from the words of this poem to describe the affections between loved ones missing each other. A loved one missing their beloved can be heard saying, *yi ri bu jian, ru ge san qiu*, meaning a day without seeing you is just like three seasons.

The original version of the title to Book VI, being The Odes of the Royal Doman, was referring to Wang or King Wang.

> By Wang (King or King's) we are to under-
> stand the territory which constituted the
> royal domain or state, attached to Loh, or
> the eastern capital of Chow [Zhou]...From
> this time the kings of Chow [Zhou] sank
> nearly to the level of princes of the States;
> and the poems collected in their domain
> were classed among the 'Lessons of Man-
> ners,' though still distinguishable by the
> epithet of 'Royal,' prefixed to them (Legge,
> 1994).

The political and philosophical significance of *Cai Ge* is that it again reminds one of the great contributions of the *Shijing* in the history of China (Yang, 1958). However, the philosophical, historical, political, and economic dimensions, rather than Romanticism, do not take away from the fact the ode of *Cai Ge* is, and will always be a simple love story. It remains the simple story of a woman that longs for the soci-ety of the object of her affections. "The lady fancies her lover engaged as the first lines describe, and would fain go and join him in his occupations" (Legge, 1994).

A final example of one of these poems or odes is *Yay Yew Man Ts'aou* (*Yi You Man Cao*), which also comes form Part I,

Eggs under a Red Flag

Lessons from the States, in Book VII, The Odes of Ch'ing (The Odes of Zheng). An English translation of *Yi You Man Cao* (Legge, 1994) follows.

> On the moor is the creeping grass,
> And how heavily is it loaded with dew!
> There was a beautiful man,
> Lovely, with clear eyes and fine forehead!
> We met together accidentally,
>
> An so my desire was satisfied.
>
> On the moor is the creeping grass,
> Heavily covered with dew.
> There was a beautiful man,
> Lovely, with clear eyes and fine forehead!
> We met together accidentally,
> And he and I were happy together.

The language of *Putonghua* (Mandarin or *Pinyin*) translation of *Yi You Man Cao* follows.

> *Ye you mancao*
> *Ling lu qing xi*
> *You mei yi ren*
> *Qing yang wan xi*
> *Qiehou xiangyu*
> *Shi wo gu xi.*
>
> *Ye you mancao*
> *Ling lu rang rang*
> *You mei yi ren*
> *Wan ru qing yang*

Lyrics of Lost Love

Xiehou xiangyu
Yu zi xie cang.[7]

The poem, *Yi You Man Cao*, uses a young woman as the main character. It is a love story about love at first sight. After meeting accidentally, they experienced a mutual attraction and were happy together. They are together simply because they were attracted to each other. It is quite simple and pure like nature itself. From the poem, we can feel the affections of the young man and young woman. We can read from this poem that at the instant moment in time that the two meet, there is a certain and good chemistry between the two lovers. It is a mutual attraction, if not love, which can be seen in their eyes. They fell in love with each other. Moreover, it was a true love, because it was truly unconditional love.

The poem tells about us both nature and love, because it describes the nature of love. When they met, their spirits and minds conjoined, perhaps not like the other animals in nature's domain, when lust is so important. It is also in the poem that we can find a hint of humanism struggling against social conventions of the time. The poem connotes respect for individuals and nature. It also connotes the encouragement of individuals to pursue their own self-identities such as the integrity of one's own mind, perhaps even spirit. Nonetheless, it remains a love poem about real love, especially unconditional love and love at first sight.

However, this ode, although clearly about two people falling in love after accidentally meeting, is, like other odes in the *Shijing*, subject to the issues of translation and interpretation. The interpretations vary; from "a lady rejoices in an

---

[7] Author's *Pinyin* translation of *Yi You Man Cao*.

unlawful connection which she had formed;" to the expressed wishes of bachelors and spinsters of the Zheng to get married in any way, because "the disorders of the state have made them pass the flower of their age unmarried," and other interpretations. Han Ying is even said to have put this ode in the mount of Confucius, "to illustrate the accidental meeting of himself and another worthy" (Legge, 1994). Nonetheless, the ode remains a love poem about the simple event of a man and woman finding love by an accidental meeting.

During the period that the poems contained in the *Shijing* were authored, one could arguably surmise that there existed greater social equality between men and woman than in other periods such as the Early, Middle, and Late Middle Ages. The poems suggest that young women could at least express theirs feelings and emotions such as love, and even their expectations of life. Perhaps the era of this poetry reflects a change in history, especially a transition to more conventional morals such as traditional Confucian ideas.

This is because women of this period arguably were not so bound to a duty of procreation and continuing the family clan, at least to the same extent as that of subsequent periods to come. It should be noted, as earlier mentioned in Chapter Five, the *Liji's Hunyi* defines marriage as the greater good (*summun bonum*) of man and woman. It is an ideal based on marriage as being a duty to worship the temple of the clan and sustain your family tree, which constitutes filial piety (*xiao shun*) (Fung, 1991).

One has to be reminded that the period of these writings either preceded or correspond with an early development of Confucianism, or the Confucian school of thought, and other competing philosophical ideals, which would gather greater momentum during and after the Spring and Autumn period. In subsequent periods to come, women would not enjoy the same freedoms of expression. One wonders if modern Chinese women and women of subsequent periods in history will ever return to the same state of freedom as demonstrated by the poems contained in the *Shijing.*

As previously discussed in Chapter Six, there was the first Chinese Renaissance and then second Chinese Renaissance in Chinese history, with the later paralleling the New Cultural Movement. The first Chinese Renaissance was an attempt to forge a greater humanism in society, resulting in greater expressions of the individual and their feelings and beliefs. However, as a movement toward greater humanism it failed. It also did not seem to substantially contribution to a freer and greater freedom of expression for women.

Nonetheless, there were benefits stemming from this glitz in dynastic or imperial history, which were really a greater freedom of expression for men, but not for women. For instance, there are the classic short-novels of *Jin Ping Mei (Jin Pingmei)* (i.e., English translations: *The Plum in the Golden Vase* or *The Golden Lotus*) (Roy, 1997; Roy, 2001), which is attributed to Lanling Xiaoxiao Sheng during Wan Li's reign of the Ming Dynasty (1368-1644), and *Yv Pu Tuan (Jou Pu Tuan)* (*The Prayer Mat of Flesh*) by Li Yu (1611-1680 A.D.) (Martin, 1963).

In these classic novels, some of which were risqué for their periods, we continue the theme of man consuming woman, especially her spirit. As earlier mentioned in Chapter Six, a problem of these classic tales or stories, like the tales of ghost, vixens, and "fox spirits," is that they emphasize the subjects of lust and a beautiful woman, but not love. These novels were typical of an earlier period, because the spirit of woman continued to be demoralized.

Eggs under a Red Flag

The novel *Jin Ping Mei* is one the five Chinese classic novels, which include, *Xi You Ji* (i.e., English translations: *Journey to the West* or *The Monkey King*); *Shuihu Zhuan* (i.e., English translations: *Water Marin* or *Outlaws of the Marsh*); *Sanguo Yanyi* (*The Romance of the Three Kingdoms*), and *Hong Lou Meng* (*A Dream of the Red Chamber*). However, *Jin Ping Mei* is distinguishable because it contains erotica, or as described by many, it may simply be excessively pornographic in its descriptions. Moreover, one source regarding *Jin Ping Mei* argues, it "is the equation of woman with sex and evil-- epitomized by the yinfu, or 'lascivious woman,' the ultimate embodiment of which is, in turn, Pan Jinlian."

Further observing, "before coming to stand for 'woman,' Pan Jinlian is a woman of a specific social status: a bondmaid-concubine, that is, a category of labor that became much more affordable and widespread in the late-Ming market economy. It is this woman of base legal condition, able to rely only on her beauty and reproductive potentiality to secure a more stable position within the family and society" (Vitiello, 2003; Ding, 2002; Edwards, 2003). It is a world of unrelenting misogyny where a man's relationships with women and animals continue to be dominated by cruelty, disdain, and the brutal exercise of powers—the world of *Jin Ping Mei*.

Louise Edwards (2003) on the subject of studying *Jin Ping Mei*, when writing a review of Ding Naifei's *Obscene Things: Sexual Politics in Jin Ping Mei* (2002), made the following observation.

> Accordingly, Ding's study of this complex novel commences with an examination of her status as a female researcher of an 'obscene book.' She explains that over the

centuries, 'legitimate' study of this book has been the preserve of the male/intellectual in an assertion of his sex and class status... Ding's central thesis emerges: 'That obscenity in the text and generations of readings has more to do with a misogynist morality that is shared in varying and different degrees by the text and readers alike. Neither authorial intention nor textual essence imparts its obscenity to the text. Rather, the latter is the joint product of complicit textual and reading processes. Misogyny is the thread that has held the readers and the novel together over centuries.'

Central to the theme of *Jing Ping Mei* is the rise to power and wealth, and the eventual death of Ximen Qing. It presents a world of evil willingly engulfed by a ruling social class, while exposing the worst side of human nature such as the harsh oppression and exploitation of common people by Ximen Qing and other officials. Although Ximen Qing has a wife and two concubines, he also later develops immoral relations with Meng Yulou, Li Ping'er, and the coquettish Pan Jinlian. Ximen Qing also eventually takes the latter three as new concubines. However, in pursuit of satisfying his sexual hunger, he also seduces his slave girl, Chunmei.

The novel *Jin Ping mei* takes its name from the three central characters, who are Pan *Jin*lian; Li *Ping*'er, one of his concubines; and Peng Chun*mei*, a maid who eventually rose to power within the family. Although Ximen Qing is the central character in this novel, the story of the domestic sexual struggles of the women fighting for influence as the power of the Ximen clan gradually declines, challenges Ximen as

the central character of the novel. *Jing Ping Mei* has been re-
nowned for centuries as pornographic material and, in the
past, has even been official banned because of its very
graphic sexual descriptions.

Many critics, however, argue that the graphic sexual descriptions are essential to the storyline, while others hail its
liberating influence on other Chinese novels in matters of
sexuality such as the *Dream of the Red Chamber* or *A Dream of
the Red Mansion* (Cao et al., 2001). However, assuming *Ji Ping
Mei* is truly either excessive erotica or pornography, it presents issues of liberating who, and how could such literature
advance the cause of the Chinese woman in both antiquity
and modernity? In terms of liberating the Chinese woman,
especially in periods to follow, *Jin Ping Mei* arguably may or
may not have advanced her cause, but one suspects that it
may have done more harm, than good.

In the 20th century, there were two key periods deserving
our attention. One is the second Chinese Renaissance
(*Zhongguo De Wenyi Fuxing*). The second is the Great Cultural
Revolution (*Wenhua Da Geming*) (1966-1976). As previously
mentioned in Chapter Six, following the May 4, 1919
Movement (*Wu Shi Yundong*), the works of writers of this
gathering turned toward critical realism with a strong social
commentary. *Art-for-art's-sake* turned toward *art-for-society's
sake*, with critical realism at the helm until the 1940s. It is a
period associated with a greater freedom of expression and
drive toward greater humanism in society. Scholars and social reformers of this period imported Western concepts of
liberty and freedom. However, they would face the barrier
of the Chinese language, especially written language, being
the Chinese character.

For instance, when importing the Western concept of liberty, rather than perhaps devise a new word in their native

language, they simply assigned it to the word (or characters), *ziyou*. While *ziyou* did mean liberty, it did not connote the Western concept of liberty. For the ordinary citizen and Chinese language, *ziyou* actually only conveyed a more limited, and non-political, meaning such as the most mundane idea of being free to do something. More accurately, the barriers were the language and culture or the language nuances of Chinese culture.

There is also the issue of the persistence of traditional Chinese culture (primarily traditional Confucianism). As these scholars and men of literature outwardly struggled to define a new liberty and freedom for China, they also found themselves caught in a struggle between new ideas such as liberty, and traditional culture. Notwithstanding an examination of their own personal lives, history may have witnessed a struggle between the grandest ideas and the nemesis of Confucianism and paternalism in their writings. In their writings, they seemingly remained silently faithful to traditional culture and paternalism.

For instance, a woman author named Xiao Hong was a good friend of Lu Xun. On one occasion, she told Lu Xun that the most miserable and unfortunate thing in her life was being a woman. While being so close to the center of the Renaissance, being the famous Lu Xun, she could not find hope for tomorrow, which she sought in desperation.

Near the waning period of the second Chinese Renaissance in the 1940s, there is a novel written by Ch'ien Chung-shu, which is entitled *Wei Cheng (Fortress Besieged)*. The book was written in 1946, and perhaps represents or symbolizes the Chinese Renaissance man's struggle between higher ideals of liberty and freedom, and those of traditional culture and paternalism In *Fortress Besieged*, the author supposedly presents a picture of a modern Chinese man (Ch'ien, 1946).

The central character is Fang Hung-chien (or Fang Hong Jian), who is best described as numb in feelings and emotions, and even cowardice. Perhaps he is the fortress yet to be besieged. Fang throughout the novel seems neither happy, nor really unhappy.

In the opening chapter of the novel, his father admonishes him for ignoring his filial duties. Then later, in a letter to his father, Fang wrote,

> A feeling of 'autumnal melancholy' has suddenly possessed me, and every time I look into the mirror at my own reflection, so gaunt and dispirited, I feel it is not the face of one destined for longevity. I'm afraid my body can't hold up much longer, and I may be the cause of a lifetime of regret for Miss Chou."

In reply, Fang's father wrote,

> If you devoted yourself to your studies as you should, would you still have the leisure to look in a mirror? You are not a woman, so what need do you have of a mirror? That sort of thing is for actors only. A real man gazes at himself in the mirror will only be scorned by society. Never had I thought once you parted from me that you would pick up such base habits. Most deplorable and disgusting! Moreover, it is said that "When one's parents are still living, a son should not speak of getting old." You have no consideration for your parents, who hold

you dearly in their hearts, but frighten them
with the talk of death. This is certainly ne-
glected of your filial duties to the extreme!
(Ch'ien, 1946).

In quick reply, Fang begged for forgiveness from his father, when trying to explain that "the mirror was his
roommate's and not something he had bought himself." In
another instance, Fang, by a letter to his father, also wanted
to escape from the obligations of a pre-arranged marriage
with Shu-ying. Before graduating from high school, Chou
(or Zhou), who was the father of Shu-ying, met with Fang's
father, which results in the two becoming friends and also
intended in-laws, even though Fang and Shu-ling had never
met. After graduation, their fathers intended for them to
marry. It was also during this time that Fang began to read
Schopenhauer and would often say to his classmates,
"Where is romantic love in the world. It's entirely the reproductive urge" (Ch'ien, 1946).

This novel mostly centers on Fang Hong-chien, by focusing on his relations to women, a continuum of lost jobs, and
other sad events. As the story starts, he was given an opportunity to go to Beijing to further his college studies. He is
living in Shanghai. His fiancé's father, Chou, had given him
money to continue his studies. The problem is that Fang
disliked his fiancée, Shu-ying. However, the two never marry
because his fiancé, Shu-ying, died. Despite the fact that Fang
will not become his son in law, his former father-in-law,
Chou, still wants to help Fang, so he gives him money to go
study abroad. Fang left Shangai and took a ship to Europe.

When in Europe, however, Fang did not study, rather he
spent or wasted his time playing. Fang's only worry is that
his money will soon run out, and he has nothing to show for

his time and expenses, especially a diploma. He eventually takes a ship to the United States, and while there he meets a questionable character that sells him a fake diploma. From the United States, he returns to Europe, and then returns to Shanghai. During the voyage to Shanghai, he met a woman, who was engaged to soon be married. This inconvenience did not stop him have enjoying a one-night stand with her. During the same time, he meets another woman, who has a PhD and is from Shanghai, and who has fallen in love with him. This inconvenience also did not distract Fang from continuing to play with his one-night stand.

Fortunately for Fang, the woman with the PhD forgives him for his promiscuousness and still wants to spend time with him after they arrive in Shanghai. In Shanghai, Fang did continue to see her. He also started working for his former father-in-law. Although during this time he is still seeing the woman with the PhD, he later meets her cousin and claims a deep love for her. The latter, however, would be another short-lived relationship because they soon broke-up due to a misunderstanding. At this time, he is still living in the home of his deceased fiancée. Fang now claims that his broken heart makes him feel so lost, and that it upsets his ex-mother-in-law to see him in this state (Ch'ien, 1946).

Fang eventually decides to leave his ex-fiancée's house, and returns to his father's house in Shanghai. A friend helps him find a job teaching at a college in another province. Fang, of course, met a young woman on the way to his new job, who falls in love with him. Fang marries her. However, Fang, in his mind, always thought that she had set a trap for him to marry her. He eventually tires of her, marriage, and life in general. Fang seems without hope. In *Fortress Besieged*, Fang Hong-chien had little patience for life, study, his job, his wife, and all of the other women in his life. In the concluding pages, he is alone, without a job, his wife left him, and he is totally lost. His plight and mind-set seems little different from the despair of Xiao Hong. Neither Fang Hong-chien, nor Xiao Hong could see hope waiting for them around the next corner.

As earlier mentioned, *Fortress Besieged* was written in 1941 by male author Ch'ien Chung-shu. In American, there was a novel written during the same period, although a decade earlier, in 1936, by a female writer, Margaret Mitchell, who wrote the famous novel of *Gone with the Wind*. While these books were authored during about the same period, there is a gravely distinguishable difference between the two novels. Notwithstanding issue of Chinese culture and Western culture, the two novels offer contrasting viewpoints of a man and woman's perspective about struggling to "make life."

There is also the earlier Chinese movie that is titled "Tempress Moon," which some find comparable to both the book and move, *Gone with the Wind*. Stephen Holden (1996) of *The New Times* wrote a movie review about "Tempest Moon," and hailed it as the Chinese "Gone with the Wind." He titled his review as "Gone with the Wind, Without War." Holden summarized the movie as "a dreamy erotic reverie on sexual politics and psychology, a Chinese 'Gone with the Wind,' without a civil war." In two of his comparisons with *Gone with the Wind*, he wrote the following.

> Near the end of the film, in a neat twist on "Gone with the Wind," it is a woman who brushes off her former lover with the equivalent of Rhett Butler's "Frankly, my dear, I don't give a damn." Otherwise, the film's portrayal of the battle of the sexes is a stereotypically melodramatic one in which

distraught women hysterically throw themselves at the coldhearted men who ravish
them. For all the buckets of tears that are
spilled, "Temptress Moon" isn't emotionally
gripping. It has the feel of a chic, kink-
ornamented romantic pageant, unfolding at
a distance.

The Scarlett and Rhett of this estheticized
soap opera are Ruyi (Gong Li) and Zhongli-
ang (Leslie Cheung), who grew up together
in the shadowy ancestral palace of the Pang
family (the movie's equivalent of Tara) outside Shanghai. Ruyi is a teen-ager when her
opium-addicted father dies and she is forced
to become the official head of the Pang
clan. Her brother, Zhengda (Zhou Ye-
mang), who was to have assumed power,
has fallen mysteriously ill and is apparently
brain dead. Both Zhengda and Ruyi were in-
troduced to opium by their father as
children (Holden, 1996).

The comparisons and similarities made by Holden (1996)
clearly share a commonality of the desire of people to simply "make life." Moreover, in the United States the release
of the movie coincides with the outbreak of war. Although
the setting for *Gone with the Wind* was antebellum and post-
antebellum South, its opening at movie theatres corre-
sponded with the first few months of the outbreak of WWII

in Europe, thus, helping Americans identify with the war story, especially the theme of survival.[8]

In *Gone with the Wind*, the central character is Scarlett O'Hara. As the novel opens, we read, "Scarlett O'Hara was not beautiful, but men seldom realized it when caught by her charm as the Tarleton twins were." In this great classic, Scarlett has to struggle with life and the paternalistic culture of the old south. In the midst of war, it was tough times for Scarlett. Nonetheless, when we read *Gone with the Wind*, we are moved by her drive, ambition, and hope. From beginning to end, in Scarlett, we see hope, resilience, and the ever-present fortitude of the human heart. The same is true of the final closing words (or lines) of the novel, when Scarlett says, "I'll think of it tomorrow, at Tara. I can stand it then. Tomorrow, I'll think of some way to get him back. After all, tomorrow is another day" (Mitchell, 1993).

Conversely, in the final pages of *Fortress Besieged*, the author abandons his central character, Fang Hong-chien. At this point of the storyline, if the author intended hope it is feigned hope. Fang is left utterly destitute in the end. He is without a job, without money, hungry, his wife left him because of his rudeness, and soon he will not have a place to live. Fang is a sad and troubled person without a symbolic "Tara," which furnished Scarlett with something to compel her to a hope for tomorrow. He lived life one disaster after the next. In the final moments of the novel, as he finds himself alone, he contemplates as follows.

> Hong-chien's nerves were too numb as he left the house to feel the cold. He was con-

8 *See* the movie review of the movie *Gone with the Wind*, http://www.filmsite.org/gone.html.

> scious only of a burning in his left cheek.
> His thoughts churned chaotically in his
> brain like snowflakes whirling about in the
> north wind. He let his legs carry him where
> they would. The all-night street lights passed
> his shadow along from one lamp to the
> next. Another self inside him seemed to be
> saying, It's all over! All over! (Ch'ien, 1946).

In the final analysis, we only come to know that his life is sad, but perhaps deservingly sad. Additionally, in the Preface to his book, the author indicates that he intended to write about a segment of modern China. However, and troubling, is that he reminds us not to forget that these characters are human beings, but "still human beings with the basic nature of hairless, two-legged animals." It is small wonder that his central character was impoverished in all the ways of being poor, which are, for instance, the ways of life, love, wealth, happiness, and humanity.

Admittedly, the setting of war torn China, especially the Japanese occupation of Shanghai, which is during the 1940s, may be good reason for this stoic outlook on life. In particular, the setting seems centered around Fang Hong-chien continually leaving and returning to China, which is in the wake of a chain of disasters. Nonetheless, if the author intended to portray a picture of the influence of modernity on the modern Chinese man, then he leaves us little hope, especially for women, in their dealings with a character such a man described as Fang Hong-chien.

The character of Fang Hong-chien also reminds one of the Confucian ideal of the benevolent man, especially the Confucian notion embodied by the statement, "meeting of himself and another worthy" (Legge, 1994). As earlier discussed, Confucius's social philosophy, in part, revolved around the concept of *ren*, which is essentially the notion of "compassion" or "loving others." One should cultivate and practice these concerns for others, and doing so required one to essentially deprecate himself. One could only do so by avoiding "artful speech" or an "ingratiating manner," which create false impressions, while also leading to self-aggrandizement. In the end, for those who managed to cultivate *ren* are the "simple in manner and slow of speech." Moreover, Confucius taught that if one failed to cultivate and practice this acute sense of the well-being and interests of others, his ceremonial manners would signify nothing (Yang, 1958).

The rudeness of Fang Hong-chien typified a man that fails to cultivate and practice this keen sense of the well-being and interests of others, as shown by his rudeness to his own family, friends, and the many women whose lives he made worst, including his wife. He is lost in two worlds, both antiquity and modernity.

Although the second Chinese Renaissance floundered during the 1940s, the scholars and men of literature did attempt to contribute to the greater freedoms of women. A contrasting period is the Great Culture Revolution, although for different reasons. Despite the travesties of the Revolution, it was during this period that woman also seemingly experienced a greater degree of social equality with men. Mao Zedong said, "Times have changed, man and woman are the same. Woman can hold half the sky." It was a period that allowed women to have more jobs than ever before. Women would do the same work as that of the men, while even dressing like the men. They were supposed to be as strong as the men, and as tough as the men. During the

Eggs under a Red Flag

Great Cultural Revolution, there was a folk song of the period, and the song begins with these words.

> We are all iron girls,
> Iron hands, iron feet, iron shoulders

> *Women doushi tie gunian*
> *tie shou, tie jiao, tie jianbang*[9]

As expressed in the opening words of the song, women would have to work like men. They drove the trucks, drove the tractors, dug the irrigation ditches, and climbed the platforms to set up electrical works, worked iron ores, and any other physical work that normally associates with men. This period witnessed not only the changing role of woman, but also a role that countered a stereotypical history of the Chinese woman. A uniqueness of the period is that political needs dictated an emphasis on social equality between man and women.

As previously mentioned, one wonders if modern Chinese women, the 21st century women, will ever return to the same state of freedom and freedom of expression demonstrated by the poems contained in the *Shijing*. For instance, in 2003, a twenty-five-year-old man claimed that he, because of successful business ventures, had accumulated vast property worth about 100,000,000 yuan.[10] In search of a wife, he placed a personal ad in sixteen different newspapers. He described himself as a male, forty-one years of age, divorced, director of private company, M.B.A. degree, 100,000,000

---

[9] Author's *Pinyin* translation.
[10] A "yuan" is the basic unit of money in China.

yuan, handsome, extraordinary, physically fit and enjoys traveling.

He further added that the woman should be less than thirty years of age, unmarried, a height of 1.62 – 1.70 meters tall, college degree of above, knowledgeable, beautiful, elegant, gentle and caring. In his personal ad, he also hints that he is searching for a virgin, by indicating "no sexual experience." Impliedly, those "of sexual experience" need not apply. Further, he indicated that anyone who is fails to fit any of the conditions should not bother him. He also did not want to be contacted by any members of the media, marriage brokers, and marriage agents. Their responses were also required to be limited by postal services and email, specifically those interested should not attempt telephone contact or, simply, drop in to meet him.

One day in July of 2003, he received several thousand responses from women. Four hundred of these responses were from one community, being Chongqing, in Sichuan Province. This personal ad received responses from both interested women and the public. What ensued were public discussions concerning his ads and the responses from women. Many thought that something must be wrong with this rich businessperson. It just seems odd that a wealthy businessperson in search of a wife would use these means, especially the posting of his personal ad and the conditions that he described.

His personal ad tells us that love is not a condition and arguably love is not a condition of marriage. What his personal ad conveys is that he is searching for the perfect woman, as described by him. He attempts to describe himself in the personal ad as the perfect man, and seeks in his mate, what he deems the perfect woman. Impliedly, this would constitute a perfect marriage. If there is any love in this sort of pre-arranged marriage, and the ways of arranging such marriages vary, it is conditional love, and not unconditional love. It is a modern day example of "love lost."

There is also the problem of thousands of women responding to this personal ad. These women, like the wealthy businessperson, obviously deemed themselves as fitting the conditions of the personal ad. Perhaps they also considered themselves the ideal perfect woman, who had now found their ideal perfect man. The implications are many. By virtue of responding to the personal ad, we can reasonably assume that these women would also deem such as a marriage as the ideal perfect marriage. It presents a crisis, because love is not a condition and equally so love is not a condition of marriage.

These women have in effect treated themselves as products in this bargaining for a contract of marriage. It is seemingly no more than another day at the office or business as usual for these women. A contract void of feelings and emotions, especially love, is no less different than a contract for a crate of widgets, which, in this instance, is a bargaining only lacking in a specified price. Their prices may be high or low, which really does not matters, because the greater concern is that they are willing to bargain themselves as products for an anticipated money profit. Perhaps the beauty of a woman is priceless, but their deeds seemingly render the value of a beautiful woman as worthless, and once again, remind us of love lost. As Mao Zedong once said, "Time changes, men and women are the same," but actually time changes, and nothing changes.

Finally, in terms of lost love, the second wife phenomenon in China also deserves mention. This is because the phenomenon has nothing to do with love and actually serves as an exemplar of lost love.

Lyrics of Lost Love

On a spring day in 2003, on a Friday afternoon when leaving Hong Kong, and in the company of a friend, a taxi was hailed down and directed him to go the Kowloon railway station. The taxi-driver was very excited. As he drove, he spoke on the taxi's cb-radio. He turned and asked where we were from. We answered, though dishonestly, Shenzhen. The driver said he will also go to Shenzhen tonight to visit his second-wife (*er nai*). He said, all of his friends have a second wife in Shenzhen, and they will all go to Shenzhen tonight. We asked, if all of his friends were taxi-drivers. He replied that not all of them were taxi-drivers, some were truck drivers. As he found that we became increasingly interested in his story about a second wife, he started to talk more about his own story. He said that his second wife was a worker in a shoe manufacturing plant. She earned about 600 rmb each month at the plant.

One time a friend, who is a second wife visited her (i.e., his second wife) and told her that each month she gets 2000 rmb from her husband. This money does not include rent, water, and electricity (utilities). She does not want to work at the plant anymore. The driver also said that her friend's husband is his friend. He said that one time the four of them went to dinner together and then after dinner they went out for karaoke. Now, they all rent an apartment in the same village on the outskirts of Shenzhen.

We asked him, how old is she? He said she is 21 years old. The driver looks about 45 or more years of age. We commented that she is so young of age and that he must love her very much. He said she is not that great. He then proceeded to announce that he actually wants to find a new second wife. We asked him if his wife in Hong Kong knew about his second wife. He said of course that my wife does not know about this. My friends and I go to Shenzhen to have food and fun, and the money spent on her would only be enough for a good meal in Hong Kong. He said that a lot of taxi drivers and truck drivers have a second wife in Shenzhen.

There are actually smaller villages where only second wives and their families live. It should also be understood that they are never legally married to these second wives. The situation of the women or these second wives is a sad state of affairs, especially for the child or children of these unconventional arrangements. When passing through the Shenzhen train station, one can observe these second wives standing outside the station waiting for their husbands.

The conversation with the taxi driver occurred in 2003, so there is a possibility that the practice of a second wife may have diminished or may occur with less frequency. Nonetheless, when traveling to or through Shenzhen via the train, one can still witness lost love or those women standing at the station alone and normally with a young child in their arms waiting for their lost love.

The Faces of Ping-Pong

On the subject of China or seemingly endless search to know and understand China, generally, many Westerners seem bound by many preconceived notions, ideas, prejudices, and biases. Images of old still haunt the minds of many Westerners as they now find themselves having to consider what to make of the new China and the Chinese people. Many will simply view modern China and the Chinese people in terms of politics or Western-inspired definitions of democracy or liberal democracy. For these people, they are simply the Chinese communists.

Others, perhaps more wisely, will see the typical Chinese person or citizen in a light reflective of images of the "old" China, which many Westerners associate with a China of an earlier age, perhaps an earlier era of a Western-inspired Romanticism. The latter perspective also has the potential of forcing us to view "others" on a people-to people basis rather than government-to-government basis, thereby potentially avoiding the pitfalls of competing notions of nationalism and ideologies.

Whatever the perspectives, though there may be many other perspectives, the West, at least typical Westerners, seems still positioned at the lower end of the learning curve of knowing and understanding both the "old" and "new" China, including the people of China. There is much that Westerners still seem not to know and understand about China and the Chinese people.

Notwithstanding the politics of the World War II, the post-World War II, and cold war eras, the 1949 founding of modern China, and earlier provocations by both the United States and China, it seems that progress was only recently made on the learning curve of knowing and understanding China and the Chinese people, which was due to a seemingly innocuous contest of table tennis or ping-pong between the Chinese and American ping-pong teams.

For many, especially Westerners, the very mention of the sport or contest of ping-pong or table tennis conjures an image or vision of the Chinese ping-pong player extraordinaire. It is perhaps an image mostly attributable to the display of skills and talents by Chinese players extraordinaire at the World Olympics and World Table Tennis Championships.

Most will arguably agree that stereotypes and formulaic conceptions of "others" and the "other world", which are admittedly good or bad, and true or false, are seemingly a historical fact of social reality. Assuming that every position or hypothesis has both a thesis and anti-thesis, despite other logical possibilities or even probabilities, we, as a modern society or the Great Society seem to have historically witnessed and suffered the worst consequences of this proclivity toward formulaic conceptions of "others" and the "other world."

On the lighter side of obvious stereotypes, or the seemingly less harmful rather than more harmful side effects of these formulaic conceptions, for some it brings to mind memories of the popular 1994 movie Forrest Gump. As most will recall, actor Tom Hanks played the role of Forrest Gump and entertained us to no end, especially with his comical images of Forrest Gump playing ping-pong. This movie enjoyed such popularity that it resulted in the interesting phenomenon of a Google search of the terms -- ping-pong and China – producing search results for Forrest Gump. An earlier Google search actually produced about 1,870,000 hits, which covers a range from general knowledge about ping-pong, ping-pong diplomacy, Forrest Gump, to even YouTube (youtube.com) videos, including a "rap" video titled "China Loves Ping Pong." In this respect, ping-pong, at least for Western eyes, may not be such an important sporting event or game of contest.

In terms of our metaphorical learning curve of knowing and understanding, though those formulaic conceptions of "others" and the "other world" remain a problem, there may be good or bad consequences that attach to associating the ping-pong player extraordinaire with a Chinese face. After-all, it seems to be tacitly assumed, though Hegel would have insisted in his search for the "more perfect" by means of conflict-induced change, that every thesis enjoys its own anti-thesis.

Nonetheless, and despite the latter, ping-pong, eventually, produces a phenomenon in the international community, which seems unmatched or unrivaled by any other sporting events or games of contest. This is because, for a brief moment in history, during the era of Mao Zedong and the presidency of Richard Milhous Nixon (presidency from 1969-1974), the sport of ping-pong was elevated to international diplomatic status, in both the United States and China.

For instance, this earlier period births the term of "ping-pong diplomacy," when, on April 10, 1971, the American ping-pong team arrives in China. Many associate the April 6, 1971-Chinese invitation to the American ping-pong team to visit China as a historic hint of improved U.S.-China relations. Moreover, during the 1970s, it may have been a Chinese initiative, and not necessarily successful cold war politics and the global balance of powers fostering improved U.S.-China relations.

Leaving one to wonder, especially in light of the U.S.-led wars in North Korea (1951), Vietnam (1961) and Grenada (1983), which were followed by Libya, Panama, the Gulf War, Kosovo, Afghanistan and Iraq, what, if anything, the United States and its allies learned from this historic international event, especially concerning the merits of soft power over hard power in the international community. In this respect, and crudely paraphrasing Joseph Nye's (1991) concept of soft power, this soft power (i.e., social, political and economic coercion) serves as the anti-thesis to military power, or simply, the threat of war.

Time magazine, a weekly American news magazine, aptly spoke of the historical significance of this contest of ping-pong when coining the phrase "the ping heard around the world," which is attributable to the then elevation of the sport of ping-pong as a tool of international diplomacy. The term of "ping-pong diplomacy" is primarily associated with the American ping-pong players being the first Americans allowed entry to China since 1949. Then following the American ping-pong team's visit, U.S. president Nixon sent

The Faces of Ping-Pong

Secretary of State Henry Kissinger to Beijing to arrange a presidential visit. In February of 1972, Nixon made a historic visit to China. Then China premier Chou En-lai (Zhou Enlai) noted that this is the first time in history that a sport was so effective in international diplomacy.

For Nixon, it was no less an important event, and reportedly, he characterized this contest of ping-pong between the two countries as a world changing event. What followed between the United States and China were improved diplomatic relations and even improved trade relations. There also followed China's improved diplomatic and trade relations with other Western countries. For better or for worse, the sport of ping-pong played a critical role in first fostering improved U.S.-China relations and then helping to open China to a Western world.

This historical event in U.S. diplomacy seems now largely overshadowed by the phenomenon of globalization and its attendant world shaking events, however. The accomplishments of the Nixon presidency are also overshadowed by the 1972 Watergate scandal and burglary of the Democratic National Committee headquarters, threat of impeachment by the U.S. House of Representatives, and in 1974 the first U.S. presidential resignation in U.S. history.

Then there is the former U.S. president William Jefferson "Bill" Clinton (presidency from 1993 to 2001), and his democratic administration, influencing the promotion of Permanent Normal Trade Relations (PNTR) with China as a top legislative priority, President Clinton's 1994 decision to de-link trade and human rights, and finally the 1998 decision of the U.S. Congress to substitute Normal Trade Relations (NTR) for Most Favored Nations (MFN) status. As the former maestro of the Federal Reserve Alan Greenspan would later observe, "I think Bill Clinton was the best Republican president we've had in a while" (Greenspan, 2007).

In fairness to the Nixon legacy, and both Republicans and Democrats, the resignation of Nixon in the face of the threat of impeachment for obstruction of justice in relation to the Watergate scandal must be measured against Clinton's actual impeachment by the U.S. House of Representatives for perjury and obstruction of justice in relation to a scandal with a White House intern, and subsequent acquittal by the U.S. Senate. Nonetheless, a legacy of both the Nixon and Clinton presidencies is they, though in different ways and means, served as important influences in opening the door to China.

It is also difficult to fathom how the sport or contest of ping-pong could produce such a world-shaking event. Depending on one's perspective, especially rightist versus leftist, this speaks to either the success or failure of politicians and their strategies of foreign policies, especially cold war politics and the global balance of power. This leaves one wondering why the respective leaders from these countries could not manage to bring about the same world shaking event by face-to-face dialogues or on a government-to-government basis and without a game of contest or sporting event. Depending on one's politics, or political preferences such as rightist or leftist, it is a fault attributable to either the United States or China, or even both countries.

In all honesty, the fault was attributable to both countries and their leaders. After the 1949 founding of modern China, Mao Zedong and the first generation leadership generally perceived the U.S. as a threat, or simply, as an enemy. Mao did initiate through Premier Zhou Enlai, however, the famous game or contest of ping-pong between the countries. There is also the seeming wisdom of the Nixon administration, because they did accept the invitation that led to further opening of the borders of China.

For the United States, there had always been a reluctance to engage China. For instance, during the earlier Harry S. Truman presidency (i.e., from 1945 to 1953), both Truman and his secretary of state, Dean Atchison, did want to establish diplomatic relations with China. The problem was reluctance in the U.S. Congress, strong support for Jiang Jieshi (Chiang Kai-shek), and even provocations by China. All of this frustrated earlier efforts during the Truman presidency to engage China diplomatically.

For these reasons, earlier failed diplomatic efforts at establishing diplomatic relations between these two powers are rightly attributable to both the United States and China. It is gravely doubtful, however, that the politicians on both sides of the fence (or both countries) will ever admit these truths. No doubt, the politicians from the respective sides (or countries) will only remind us of either the Western threat or Chinese threat. One suspects that the truth, as always, lies somewhere in between these corresponding threats of seemingly "other" worlds. Truth often seems not to come easy for many politicians, whether in a China polity or U.S. polity, as respective ideologies, nationalism, and the goal of staying in power or political office often overrides the domestic needs of citizens.

Moreover, form a Chinese perspective, the sport or contest of ping-pong is arguably much more than a sporting event, because the importance of ping-pong to the Chinese people is not definable solely in terms of the politics of ping-pong diplomacy. The importance of the art of ping-pong is far more reaching and broader than serving as a tool or instrument of diplomacy.

Eggs under a Red Flag

There are consequences that attach to ping-pong as a phenomenon of Chinese culture and the Chinese personality. Ping-pong may be a game or a sport, depending on the respective context of play, but it is still a sport requiring a great deal of athleticism and other skills. For the Chinese people, ping-pong is one of the country's most important and premier sports. The Chinese also enjoy other games or contests such as Chinese chess, Ma Jiang, and even the ancient Chinese board game of *Go* (or *Weiqi*). Then, there are other sports on the mainland, which Western biases and prejudices, though admittedly probably more unconsciously than consciously, often seem to ignore.

For instance, serving as a reminder to the world, especially the United States, of China's greater versatility, there was the arrival of basketball star Yao Ming at the U.S.-based National Basketball Association (NBA), which is the Houston Rockets professional basketball team. For those still harboring biases and prejudices, here was a Chinese athlete that was tall in statute and possessed more that sufficient basketball skills, which qualifies Yao Ming to join the professional ranks of the NBA. However, though a disappointment, in July of 2011, Yao announces his early retirement from the NBA, which is attributable to an injury.

There is also the 2007 NBA first round (sixth pick) draft pick of Chinese player Yi Jianlian (He Shan, China) by the Milwaukee (Wisconsin) Bucks. These other examples of the power of sports in the international arena, though not enjoying the status of ping-pong diplomacy, still serve as conscious shaking events for those who dare to harbor wrongful biases and prejudices, or those formulaic conceptions of "others" and the "other world." For many Americans, it is a problem of lack of knowing and under-

The Faces of Ping-Pong

standing, and still being at the lower end of the learning curve.

As for the game or sport of ping-pong, the Chinese people neither invented ping-pong, nor does not ping-pong originally hail from China. Many Chinese people, actually, do not know the origins of ping-ping. The game or sport of ping-pong actually comes from the British, when during the late 19th century they transformed the outdoor sport of tennis into the indoor sport of table tennis. Many Chinese think that it is of Chinese origin because of the namesake of ping-pong, which could be by virtue of the sound of the spoken words of ping-pong, which seem to resemble the sound of Chinese characters or the Chinese native language of Mandarin or *Putonghua*. In China, actually, in the national language of *Putonghua* (or Mandarin), ping-pong is the word (or characters) *ping-pang*, reflecting a non-native word borrowed from the English language.

The namesake of ping-pong, actually, has a Western origin, which is associated with the sound of "ping pong" as the ball bounces off the table and paddle. In an early era, the original equipment simply consisted of dining-room tables and balls of cork. Around the turn of the century, the game underwent a few changes in England, with first the introduction of a celluloid ball and, then later, by adding pimple-rubber to a wood paddle.

In 1900, as the technique of play developed, alongside improved technology, the material used for the ball also evolves. The product used in the construction and manufacture of the ping-pong ball changed from rubber to plastic. As a result, the plastic ball produced a ping and pong sound as it volleyed back and forth across the table, and the game or sport of table tennis became synonymous with ping-pong.

Eggs under a Red Flag

It was still an English import, however, because the game or sport of ping-pong did not make its arrival in China until 1904. This occurs when a savvy Shanghai businessman brought the first table tennis game to China, after purchasing ten sets of table tennis, including the tables and equipment. The earlier game or recreational game, however, lost some of its popularity, and it would not be until the 1920s that a new interest in the game would appear. Growing interests in the recreational game of ping-pong on the European continent would eventually, in 1926, give birth to the International Table Tennis Association (ITTF). What follows was the growing association of the recreational game of ping-pong as a sport. Subsequently, the now sport of ping pong would leave the European continent under the umbrella of the ITTF, as it soon spread to Japan and then to other Asian nations.

Following the close of World War II, the Japanese ping-pong players would dominate the sport for much of the 1950s and 1960s. However, in the 1960s and 1970s, the world witnessed Chinese players begin to close the gap and, during the 1960s and 1970s, China alone dominated the sport. It would not be until 1988 that table tennis would officially become an Olympic event. After introducing table tennis (or ping-pong) as an Olympic event, other nations such as Sweden and South Korean would join the top ranks. Nonetheless, despite the advancing ping-pong skills of athletes from other countries, the Chinese ping-pong players continue their dominance in the sport of ping-pong (or table tennis) or *ping-pang*.

Moreover, the development of ping-pong in China, arguably, corresponds with China's much-troubled history, which was a history of civil strife, civil war, and an unfamiliar, and resented, foreign presence. It was only after the emergence of the People's Republic of China (China) in 1949 that the Chinese ping-pong player extraordinaire would make his or her appearance in the world arena of sports. On April 5, 1959, China won the 25th World Ping-Pong Tournament in Germany. This was China's first world championship in sports, and China's first world championship in a sport that it would dominate in years to come.

By the time of the 2004 Athens Olympic Games, when China walked away with three out of four gold medals, China had won almost all the world titles for the past decade and 16 Olympic gold medals - including three in Athens. China's state ping-pong teams have set a standard so high that only a few nations could possibly follow such a record-setting pace. During the 2005 World Table Tennis Championships, Chinese players swept all five titles at the tournament, making China the first country to reach the 100-gold medal mark and rewriting ping-pong history. The Chinese people continue to treasure the sport of ping-pong as one of their national pastimes.

Perhaps for the Chinese people, the sport of ping-pong or *ping-pang* bears the same significance as baseball to an America public. In the United States, the sport of baseball is so prevalent that many contend that it enjoys religion dimensions. For instance, there was even an issue of the *Journal of the American Academy of Religion* that was devoted entirely to the discussion of American popular culture and religion. One of these essays was written by David Chidester, and it is titled, "The Church of Baseball, the Fetish of Coca-Cola, and the Potlatch of Rock 'n' Roll" (1996). In his article, Chidester argued for the inclusion of America's favorite pastime in the academic study of religion.

For Chidester (1996) and other scholars, the sport of baseball possesses or reflects a distinctive set of myths, rituals, and codes of behavior, which parallel the formal elements of what many deem official religions. As a parallel to so-called official religions, the sport of baseball functions to unite a community of participants/believers and orients them to a sort of atemporal social and cosmic order.

The latter, as earlier discussed in Chapter One, bears resemblance to the phenomenon of small groups in China (Jin, 2004) and the "survival in groups" instinct, especially the "way the group conceives of itself" (Morrison, 2006; Durkheim, 1938). Catherine Albanese, in her article, "Religion and American Popular Culture: An Introductory Essay" (1996), explored the perceptions of American culture and popular religion in the academy. She uniquely posited a thesis that popular religious practices and traditions do not constitute a subsidiary, primitive or low form of religion, which stands in opposition to high, ecclesiastic or official religions. Rather, according to Albanese (1996), popular religious culture necessitates alternative analytic models, in order to fully grasp the symbolic power and import that such traditions carry forth in human experiences.

Chidester (1996) builds on Albanse's theory when describing the ways that secular concepts or systems such as American baseball, the Coca-Cola soft drink, and rock and roll music possess tremendous symbolism, while also ordering communities, scared space, and time for American lives. As for baseball, which is arguably true for Chinese *ping-pang*, Chidester perceives three ways that baseball can be seen as a church of sorts. First, baseball involves tradition, heritage, and collective memory. Second, baseball creates and orders an extended community of enthusiasts that attend the same church. Third, baseball possesses a sense of normality that orders time and space, thus creating a familiar, if not near domestic, environment for its fold.

The Faces of Ping-Pong

Perhaps China's pastime of ping-pong, like American's favorite pastime of baseball, serves as a vehicle of culture, equally functioning to unite a community of participants/believers and orients them to an atemporal social and cosmic order, though one with a distinctive Chinese order. As Arthi Devarajan and Harshita Mruthinti Kamath (2009) suggested, Chidester's model of baseball is easily extendable to other American non-Christian traditions, and impliedly other non-American non-Chirstian traditions, which encompass similar elements. As a vehicle of culture, the national pastime of ping-pong is arguably no less for China. It is relevant that Mao Zedong via Zhou Enlai invited the American ping-pong team to China, rather than a team from another sport.

There is also significance attributable to China's state ping-pong teams winning a succession of medals in the sport of ping-pong in international competition such as the Beijing 2008 Olympic Games. For the Chinese people, the sport of ping-pong has served as a great source of "face" (*mian zi*) for them in the world arena. In the language of *Putonghua* (Mandarin or *Pinyin*), *mian zi* (i.e., face) means honor, whereas, the distinguishable *zhun lian* (i.e., face) connotes the process or practice of Chinese players working hard to obtain the honor that will gives *mian zi* (i.e., face) to others.

There is also an added psychological dimension to the game for the Chinese people because while many enjoy the game, or euphemistically speaking, it is everyone's game, it is still the sport of the ping-pong player extraordinaire. This is due to ping-pong consisting, in part, of athleticism, and, in part, a certain degree of mental fitness, because it is a game or sport of spin or what in the English language refers to "putting english" on the ball.

This is not the game of Forrest Gump, or someone playing the game as a sort of desiccated machine, if not in a robot-like fashion. A player must understand how to spin the ball for a given situation, and read and react to the spin that an opponent may put on the ball. You cannot simply whack the ball, because you must first figure out what is happening, what will happen, and then try to do the right thing. Sports scientists that have studied ping-pong conclude that it is one of the most difficult sports to master, which is by virtue of the demands on a player. A player must be of quick reflex, have sufficient stamina, be able to hit perfect strokes, and be able to intensely concentrate, while also being able to adjust in a split second to an ever-changing spin, speed (as fast as 1,500 rpm), and the direction of the ball.

Finally, all of which, from China's historic invitation to the U.S. ping-pong team, to the practice of Chinese people working hard to obtain the honor that will give face to others, are the faces (both *mian zi* and *zhun lian*) of *ping-pang*. The latter, although in an odd sort of way, may well symbolize the differences between China and the West.

Limited Words, but Unlimited Meanings

There are vast differences between Chinese culture and Western culture. In the West, the development of culture seems to have turned more around the struggles of religion and religious freedoms than any other forces of change; i.e. early Renaissance, the Reformation, and the Age of the Enlightenment. Historically, it is a struggle of ideas, such as issues of human rights, which are more accurately the Western Enlightenment ideas of liberty and tolerance. It was the ageless problem of the intolerance of the church, and the theological-political problem of the political authority of the church. In terms of the history of China, however, history is not caught in a similar struggle of ideals, especially Western notions of liberty, religious ideas, and the problem of the intolerance of the church.

Mao Zedong earlier described the life of the Chinese people, at least in part, as "fight with the sky, joyful; fight with the land, joyful; fight with people, joyful" (*yu tian dou, qi le wuqiong; yu di dou, qi le wuqiong; yu ren dou, qi le wuqiong*). For instance, the concept of "fight with the sky, joyful" can mean dealing with nature's storms and ill weather, while the concept of "fight with the land, joyful" may convey the struggle of harvesting crops from land. Mao's depiction is not one strongly and directly linked with higher ideas or ideals, rather it is one portraying the Chinese people as caught in the daily struggle, although an joyous struggle, of simply "making life" (*weile shenghuo*).

A distinguishing point is that while everyone has to fight with the sky and land, including even Westerners, Mao was emphasizing the aspect of "fight with people, joyful." For Mao, "fight with people, joyful" could broadly mean fight with American imperialism (*Mei de guo zhuyi*), Soviet revisionism (*Shu xiu zhuyi*), Jiang Jieshu (Chiang Kai-shek), party opponents such as *zhu ji pai* or *you pai* (rightist), or, simply, those whom he thought disagreed with him.

Chinese culture could be describable as the long historical development of the art of "fight with people, joyful." The art of "fight with people, joyful" translates into the art of dealing with people, joyful. For the Chinese people, the art of dealing with people, joyful, especially social relations, are a mainstay of Chinese culture and the Chinese family system. Oftentimes, the cultural differences between China and the West seem as broad as the Pacific Ocean.

Chinese culture and the personality are also arguably describable in terms of the game of ping-pong, because, though metaphorically speaking, the distinctiveness of both culture and the personality are akin to the game of ping-pong. For example, you cannot play ping-pong very well if you lack experience in playing the game. It is likewise true that if you have never experienced living in China, you can hardly begin to understand Chinese culture, the Chinese people, and especially the Chinese personality. It goes without saying that if you just travel to, or briefly visit, China, and not really spend time living in China, you cannot say that you know China or the Chinese people.

In China, the game of ping-pong is similar to the two-person contest in the art of Chinese *gongfu*, what Western culture euphemistically calls kung fu, especially in Western cinema. The game or sport of ping-pong, like *gongfu*, employs strategy for successful play and results. More particularly, it is a hidden and not so obvious strategy, resembling a current in a river. Although the current lies beneath the water and you cannot see it, you can feel its force and pull when attempting to forge a river or stream.

As earlier mentioned, in Chapter Eight, in the game of ping-pong, the path of the ping-pong ball is very complicated, because the movement of the ball may be fast and it may be with spin or without spin. Successful play, in part, requires serving and returning the ball, which is not a matter of simply staring at the ball, because you must a judge whether a ball in movement is with topspin, downspin, or simply, no spin at all. Complicating the game or sport are other decisions such as whether the ball is close or far from the net and whether the spin of the ball is traveling slow or fast. Further complicating the game or play is that every serve and return of the ball needs a precise spin or lack of spin. Successful play of the ping-pong ball in world-class competition is, indeed, a tour de force.

In a short movie, or video, about the making of the movie Forrest Gump, one can experience through the eyes of Forrest Gump how the actors simulate playing a world-class ping-pong match without a ball. The players supposedly get a sense of when they should be hitting the imaginary ball by listening to a metronome, as it sounds a repeated and exact tempo for them to follow. They would later digitally add the image of the ping-pong ball to the movie. Perhaps neither the movie, nor this short video serves justice to the actual skills required in this game, especially when measured by the Chinese ping-pong player extraordinaire.

The strategy involved in ping-pong, metaphorically speaking, is akin to the Chinese people when they are simply talking or trying to "make life". This is because their words can have different meanings like the spin or lack of spin on the ball. It is like the language of Chinese antiquity, the old language of China. For instance, in terms of the old language, Fung Yu-lan contended that the old language of Confucius was explainable in different context and meanings. According to Fung Yu-lan (1991), unlike Western philosophy, Chinese art, paintings, drawings, poetry and other art forms were all full of hints, requiring the trained eye to extrapolate from generalities the specific meanings.

This is because, in traditional Chinese culture, a good poem would have "limited words (or characters), but unlimited meanings" (*yan you jing yi wu qiong*). It was a lack of specifics, or generalities in want of specifics, which contributes to difficulties in translations, while also being subject to different translations or meanings. Borrowing from the title of the 2003 movie starring actor Billy Murray (playing the role of Bob Harris), we should learn to feel and read emotions, thoughts, intentions, and desires without overly expressing them, because we can become "lost in translation."

As an analogy, this viewpoint bears relevancy to some local Chinese officials (or officers), because in terms of their promptings or edicts (or rules), every sentence is correct, but useless. Generally, when questioning many of these

Limited Words, but Unlimited Meanings

Chinese officials (or officers) concerning their edicts, they respond that we must *yan jiu* (i.e., we have to discuss this or research this further), as they seldom offer a straightforward yes or no answer. For those Chinese citizens searching for the elusive yes or no answer in the promptings or edicts of local officials or officers, they typically find themselves left to guess and feel the meanings, which is arguably analogous to the game of ping-ping. Following a serve, when it comes to you, you have to guess if it has topspin, downspin or no spin. If you want to have a "smooth way" in your work, you have to prepare more than two ways to handle the way that a problem might come to you.

In China, there is a saying, *Shang you zhengce, xia you dui ce* (Above there is the policy; below there is the counter-policy), essentially meaning that there are rules, but also ways to handle things. In post-Mao China, the latter saying came about because it became commonplace for Beijing's policies to be ignored or distorted by local officials or officers, and in response, on the mainland the localities strove to find ways to get around both Beijing policies and distortions of Beijing's policies by local officials or officers. In short, preparing for a "smooth way" in your work, as in preparing for the next two steps in returning the ping-pong ball, as do the top players, you manage to obtain some control over the situation, which is assuredly to your advantage.

Chairman Mao (Mao Zedong) was the most successful in learning and using knowledge of Chinese culture and the Chinese personality. Mao once said, we should use two ways of revolution to deal with two ways of anti-revolution (*yong geming de liang shou dui fu fan geming de liang shou*). One must anticipate whatever method or tool an opponent may use, and accordingly make preparations in anticipation of these methods or tools.

Eggs Under A Red Flag

Such preparations, however, often have the unwanted effect of sometimes confusing opponents, as well as confusing allies. Perhaps in the perfect scenario, nobody knows what the genuine meanings or fake meanings are. The latter presents the problem of discerning between the imaginary and real (or genuine). It is by this method that Mao fashioned his strategies of war and life, from fighting opponents on the field of battle to, simply, "fight with people, joyful". For instance, a question yet to be resolved in China is why Mao started the Great Cultural Revolution (*Wenhua Da Geming*) (1966-1976). Mao's concept of "fight with people, joyful" arguably presents possibility of consequences yet to unfold.

Mao's war strategies, in conjunction with the previously mentioned notions of the art of ping-pong, also demonstrate the distinctiveness of Chinese culture and the Chinese personality. During the 1930s, forced by the *Kuomintang*, the Mao-led Red Army of China commences the famous 25,000-mile march (1934–35). In China, actually, the measure of a Chinese mile is a li and a li is twice the distance of a kilometer; i.e. the 25,000-mile march equals a distance of US 6,000 miles (9,660 km.). During one engagement, The Red Army marched back and forth across the same river four times. The *Kuomintang* and its military experts could not have imagined that the Red Army would march in such a fashion, which was continually crossing the same river, especially an unprecedented four times. More importantly, pursuant to this strategy, the Red Army managed to enlarge its force by a very patient and secretive way. Although in theory Mao's military practices have been cast in terms of "local war" (*jubu zhanzheng*) doctrine, or Sun Tzu's *Art of War* (1963)(*Sunzi Bingfa*), it was a strategy of preparing for a "smooth way" by preparing for the next two steps, perhaps even, metaphorically speaking, like preparing to return a served ping-pong ball.

Additionally, in August of 1940, General Peng Dehuai led the Red Army in the famous battle of *Bai Tuan Da Zhan* (100-regiment battle), which is a famous battle against the Japanese army (Xu, 2005). A month before the battle, General Peng telegraphed Mao and requested permission to execute his plan. Peng did not receive a reply from Mao, and assumed that if Mao did not say "no", he might have meant, "yes." Not hearing from Mao, Peng put into action his previously drawn plans for battle.

Although the Red Army was victorious in battle, the ensued victory dangerously served as a reminder to both the Japanese and *Kuomintang* armies that the Red Army was a large and formidable force. Consequently, they begin to put, or transferred, more forces against the Red army. General Peng Dehuai launched the *Bai Tuan Da Zhan* (100-regiment battle) and Mao criticized him harshly, during and after the Anti-Japanese War. In 1944, Mao said, "Some comrades thought the more Japanese they killed, the more patriotic they are, but they are absolutely wrong. These comrades are not our patriots; they are patriots of KMT's state. Japanese, Chiang and ourselves, we are three states."

As previously mentioned, one must anticipate whatever method or tool an opponent may use, and accordingly make preparations in anticipation of these methods or tools. However, such preparations often have the odd effect of sometimes confusing opponents, as well as confusing allies. In the case of General Peng and the 100-regiment battle, Mao's action or non-decision may have confused the opponents, the Japanese and *Kuomintang* armies, and his ally, Peng. In the aftermath, Mao was very upset with Peng's decision.

In the 1960s, during an argument with General Pang, Mao remembered this incident. In the heat of argument, Mao reminded Peng of his lack of co-operation in the past, such as his pre-emptive decision during the 100-regiment battle. Perhaps these instances reflect how Mao fashioned his strategies of war and life, from fighting opponents on the field of battle to "fight with people, joyful" or dealing with people, joyful.

Britain in the late 19th century could not have conceived of the importance to the Chinese people of transforming outside tennis into indoor table tennis or ping-pong. As previously mentioned, in Chapter Eight, China's state ping-pong teams, and their ping-pong players extraordinaire have set a standard so high that only a few nations could possibly follow such a record-setting pace. However, and more importantly, what seemingly escapes Western understanding is that the art of ping-pong, at least in China, arguably mimics the art of life, "dealing with people, joyful," or perhaps Mao's "fight with people, joyful." It is the problematic dilemma of *xu xu shi shi*, the imaginary versus real, or perhaps the question of spin or no spin on a ping-pong ball or the metaphorical ball of life.

10

Just "Making Life"

The book, as earlier mentioned in the Preface, generally addressed the topics of Chinese culture, the Chinese family system, and the Chinese people. The book intended to do so by exploring the latter topics, especially Chinese culture in general, by drawing on a diverse and varying range of resources, which range from the old or antiquity, to the new or modernity.

As also earlier mentioned, the title of the book, *Eggs under a Red Flag*, borrows from the Chinese rock 'n' roll star Cui Jian, the father of Chinese rock 'n' roll, and his 1994 song, *Hongqi Xiade Dan*. In the English language, most will translate the latterr song, the original Chinese version or *Hongqi Xiade Dan* as meaning either eggs under the red flag or balls under the red flag.[11]

---

[11] *Cui jian, Hong qi xia de dan, Pinyin* Lyrics, Copyright © 2009-2011. Azlyricdb.com;http://Pinyin.azlyricdb.com/lyrics/C/Cui-jian-Hong-qi-xia-de-dan-Pinyin-lyrics-9165.

Eggs Under A Red Flag

Then there is the primary issue of the book or the dominant theme of Chinese culture, which is distinguishable from the red culture movement, red culture campaign, or simply, what hails as red culture. This is because red culture, the red culture movement or red culture campaign is not commensurate with the themes of Chinese culture, the Chinese family system, and the Chinese people. The latter consequence is largely owing to the fact or social fact that the red culture phenomenon does not enjoy critical acceptance as an actual culture by the Chinese people, while Chinese culture does.

Red culture, the red culture movement or the red culture campaign does enjoy unique characteristics, however. The uniqueness of the red culture phenomenon lies in its relation to most, if not, all of the earlier mentioned influences, which were previously discussed in the Preface, of race, culture, nationality, and political preferences.

For instance, on July 1, 2011, the Chinese Communist Party (CCP) celebrated its 90th birthday. The celebration was a propaganda extravaganza. The events, or propaganda spectacles, celebrating the birth of the Chinese Communist Party widely ranged from impromptu singing of "Red Songs" in city squares, the relation of personal stories in China's official news media sources, "Red Movies" in local movie theatres, and even a growing interest by China's populous in tours of the hometowns of past party leaders.

As suggested by the title, *Eggs under a Red Flag*, the book addresses, although only indirectly, the importance of this fervor for red culture or what many refer to as the red culture movement or the red culture campaign. The red culture phenomenon may or may not be important. The red culture phenomenon may be able to nestle itself comfortably alongside Chinese culture. Some may even suggest, although a tenuous contention, that the red culture phenomenon may also challenge Chinese culture.

The book, however, did not undertake to explore directly the relationship or even balance between Chinese culture and red culture, the red culture movement or the red culture campaign. This is because the primary focus of the book is Chinese culture, the Chinese family system, and the Chinese people, rather than the issue of the successes of the red culture phenomenon.

For this reason, as a challenge, if any, to what generally hails as red culture, the book only indirectly challenges red culture, the red culture movement or red campaign as representing Chinese culture. This is because red culture does not represent Chinese culture per se. As many realize, the red culture movement or red campaign is a propaganda extravaganza intending to both celebrate the 90th birthday of the Chinese Communist Party (CCP), and galvanize China's populous by means of the old revolutionary ways.

Nonetheless, it is still, admittedly, difficult to deny that the red culture movement or red culture campaign is enjoying a certain degree of success or even effectiveness. This is because, since the 1920s, the phenomenon of red culture has always had a place in modern Chinese society. This is from the inception of the CCP some 90 years earlier, to the founding of modern China, to China now trying to find its place in a new global order.

In this respect, although the red culture movement or red culture campaign might not enjoy critical acceptance by the Chinese people, it still has far-reaching implications and influence. One-party rule by the CCP makes this a truism. However, notwithstanding a political-inspired red culture movement or red culture campaign, and the attendant political influence of the CCP as a certain harbinger of its successes, Chinese culture still retains its position as the most prominent and dominant force in society.

This also explains why the primary issue or dominant theme of the book is Chinese culture. In other words, and borrowing from the words of Emile Durkheim, in his classic, *Suicide, a Study in Sociology* (1951), Chinese culture is of the variety of phenomena that leads us "to know what are the facts termed 'social.'" In his classic study of suicide, Durkheim was addressing the issue of what is a social fact. More specifically, Durkheim described a social fact as "any way of acting, whether fixed or not, capable of exerting over the individual an external constraint; or: which is general over the whole of a given society whilst having an existence of its own, independent of its individual manifestations."

The dominant theme and force of Chinese culture clearly fits under the category of a social fact, or simply, what Durkheim earlier characterizes as the "facts termed 'social.'" For this reason, the underlying theme of this book or the thread that runs through each sentence, paragraph, and chapter is Chinese culture, which, in reality, constitutes the "facts termed 'social'", or simply, the social facts.

It is also for this reason that the book did not need to either directly or indirectly challenge the provenance of red culture, the red culture movement or red culture campaign. This is due to the reality that the stripping away of the powers of the CCP as a certain harbinger of the successes of the red culture phenomenon and as a linchpin for its influence would render red culture a nugatory synonym for culture or even a social fact. While red culture does not enjoy "an existence of its own, independent of its individual manifestations" (Durkheim, 1951), Chinese culture contra distinguishably clearly possess these characteristics because it is a social fact.

Just "Making Life"

The same is true about the red flag, because a flag, like the red flag or flag of the People's Republic of China is the symbol of a nation. In the context of modern China, it is actually a symbol of the CCP and the revolution. Red culture, the red culture movement or red culture campaign also serves as a symbol of the CCP. However, symbolisms such as the red flag and red culture do not symbolize Chinese culture, especially as an exemplary of what generally typifies culture per se.

Moreover, it is strongly intimated that Cui Jian, by his controversial rock 'n' roll songs, such as *Hongqi Xiade Dan* and his famous *Yi Wu Suo You* (1989) (English translations: "Nothing to My Name" or "I Have Nothing"), also did not intent to symbolize disdain for the CCP or the red flag. Notwithstanding Cui's 1989 song, *Yi Wu Suo You* ("Nothing to My Name"), becoming for many an unofficial anthem of student protestors during the era of the Tiananmen Square protests of 1989, this is because arguably a better description of his controversial rock 'n' roll songs is a symphony of feelings and aspirations for a better China, or a better world.

Then there is the issue of the meaning of the term "eggs," which, unlike the red flag and red culture, are arguably neither symbolisms (i.e., symbols of the CCP), nor ideals. When in search of a definition or definitional meaning of the word or term "eggs," in the context of *Eggs under a Red Flag*, it is admittedly difficult. This is because the possible meanings, interpretations, and translations will hardly leave us with a uniform definition. As previously mentioned in the Preface, notwithstanding typical language translation problems, the meanings and interpretations of topics in this book, including the title, remain dependent on and subject to many influences such as race, culture, nationality, and political preferences. All of which will, ultimately, presents a wide range of possible meanings and interpretations, which could range from the most innocuous meanings and interpretations, to even unspoken sensitivities. The problems that associate with language translations demonstrate this potential of diverse meanings and interpretations.

For example, in the language of Chinese culture, the title of the book, *Eggs under a Red Flag*, is an English translation of the Chinese words (or characters) *Hong qi xia de dan*.[12] In the latter, and demonstrating a potential problem with English translations, are the language nuances of Chinese culture. In the Chinese language (*Putonghua*, Mandarin or *Pinyin*), *hong* means red (color), *qi* means flag, *de dan* connotes an egg or eggs, and then, more importantly, there is the word (or character) *xia*. The latter word (or character) *xia* is important, because in the Chinese language one of the many meanings of the word (or character) *xia* is to "give birth to," as in lay eggs (Oxford University Press (China) Ltd., 1999).

Consequently, it can be said that the words, *Eggs under a Red Flag*, mean that the red flag gave birth to these eggs. In other words, they are simply the eggs birthed by the red flag. The latter meaning, interpretation, and translation, although there admittedly may be many possible meanings, interpretations, and translations, especially in other languages, demonstrate and reflect the language nuances of Chinese culture.

In yet another example, as earlier mentioned, the meanings and interpretations of his words are dependent on and subject to many influences such as race, culture, nationality, and political preferences. As previously mentioned, there are the problems of different meanings, interpretations, and translations. This is because there are the eggs, which may

---

[12] Author's *Pinyin* translation.

be good and bad eggs, good or bad eggs, similarly shaped-eggs or differently shaped-eggs, and the same or different kinds of eggs.

Granted, although not the primary focus of the book, the eggs are admittedly important, but in a different way and for other reasons. As earlier mentioned in the Preface, the title to the book itself presents an implied-query (i.e., the *petitio principii*), which begs the question – so what about Chinese culture, the Chinese family system, and the Chinese people? The book intended to keep faith with this implied query by exploring the real or genuine context of the eggs, which is primarily Chinese culture. As a consequence, a red flag is unimportant, and as for the eggs, they are only some-what important, because their importance is contingent on the real context of Chinese culture, the Chinese family system, and the Chinese people.

In other words, the importance, if any, of eggs are argua-bly contingent on them serving as a sort of representative of what constitutes Chinese culture and its many facets, which widely range from the phenomenon of the small group and social networks, to Xiao Mei's journey to retirement, the notion of a modern "fox spirit," the critical realism of the novel *Fortress Besieged*, to the faces of ping-pong. This is due to the approach and perspective of the book in trying to keep faith with the earlier mentioned implied-query (i.e., the *petitio principii* or assuming the initial point), which is Chinese culture as the undeniable initial point. Thus, in this respect, the relevancy of eggs, although admittedly an abstraction, is that they could be said to constitute or represent Chinese culture and its various facets.

For these reasons, the book also explored various (both old and new) topics of Chinese culture. While exploring these various topics, the book did attempt to introduce modern examples of old ideas, the old ways, and the traditions in antiquity, if any, that are still prevalent in society.

One could also say that this also arguably necessitated distinguishing between "the" eggs, "some" of the eggs, and "all" of the eggs. This is because the book addresses neither "the" eggs, nor "all" of the eggs, rather "some" of the eggs. For instance, as seen in Chapter One, "Something we do, not something I do," one can glean some of the eggs from the Chinese students on college campuses and their various social relations, social groups, social networks or small groups surviving via a "survival in groups" instinct. Some of the eggs are simply people or family and friends (*shu ren*) sharing Chinese dishes or being together in a small group enjoying hot pot (*huo guo*). Some of the eggs are even the criminal wrongdoing of Lu De Bin via his social network facilitating the murder of his wife.

As seen in Chapter Two, "You contain me, I contain you," some of the eggs are Madame Kuan's poem and her famous water and clay analogy; and the expectations of coaches, leaders, teachers, friends, and family, in the stadiums, classrooms, and examination rooms, including marriages and divorces.

From Chapter Three, "The Twilight Years – Xu Hang Hong," some of the eggs are Xiao Mei successfully fighting depression (*qingxu di luo*) and getting her fulcrum of life back via her social network. In the same vein, some of the eggs are also Xiao Mei and her friends listening to Russian folk songs such as Vasily Solovjev-Sedoi's *Moshike jiawai de wanshang* (*Evening in Moscow Suburbs*), and the elderly visiting public parks such as *Yue Xiu Gongyuan* (Yue Xiu Public Park) in Guangzhou, Guangdong Province for the sake of pure enjoyment and relaxation, rather than any political ideals or meanings (i.e., red culture, red culture campaign or red culture movement) that may be attributable to these songs.

In Chapter Four, "Chinese Woman, is Thy Name Frailty," Chapter Five, "Her Spirit Demoralized," and Chapter Six "Ghosts, Vixens, and 'Fox Spirits,'" there is social status of women or womanhood in both antiquity and modernity. More broadly speaking, from Chapters Four, Five, and Six, some of the eggs are seen in the works of writers, artists, painters, poets, and playwrights. For instance, from the short film Bus 44 (*Che Si Shi Si*), which was directed by Chinese-American director Dayyán Eng; the tales or dreams of ghosts, vixens, and "fox spirits" such as Xu Zhonglin's classic novel of *Fengsheng Yanyi* (*Creation of the Gods*); the classic novel of Pu Songling (1640-1715), being *Liao Zhai Zhi Yi* (i.e., English translations: *Strange Stories from a Chinese Studio* or *Fairy Ghost Vixen*); to Lady Wang's poem titled *A Plaint of Lady Wang*.

There are many examples of some of the eggs. For example, in Chapter Seven, "Lyrics of Lost Love," some of the eggs are the classical writings from the *Shijing* such as the love poems or odes *Kwan ts'eu* (*Guan Jiu*) and *Ts'ae koh* (*Cai Ge*); the classic short novel of *Jin Ping Mei*; Ch'ien Chung-shu's book *Wei Cheng* (1942) (*Fortress Beseiged*); the wealthy businessperson, who, as the epitome of lost love, places a personal advertisement seeking a mate without sexual experience for a wife and for a fee; and the second wives (*er nai*) in Shenzhen, who live in a village of second wives.

In Chapter Eight, "The Face of Ping-Pong," there is the discussion about ping-pong arguably being akin to an official religion, like baseball functions in America, by uniting a community of participants/believers, while also orienting them to a sort of atemporal social and cosmic order. The latter contention strongly resembles the phenomenon of small groups in China (Jin, 2004) and the "survival in groups" instinct, especially the "way the group conceives of itself" (Morrison, 2006; Durkheim, 1938). In Chapter Eight, there are also the faces of ping-pong, which, in the Chinese language (Mandarin or *Pinyin*), are the faces (both *mian zi* and *zhun lian*) of *ping-pang*.

Then, in Chapter Nine, "Limited Words, but Unlimited Meanings," there is a general discussion about how culture actually works, which is from getting along with others, interacting with local officers, a discussion about why Mao Zedong may have been the master of "fight with the sky, joyful; fight with the land, joyful; fight with people, joyful" (*yu tian dou, qi le wuqiong; yu di dou, qi le wuqiong; yu ren dou, qi le wuqiong*), to simply, "making life" (*weile shenghuo*).

There are also the relatively more modern works of writers, artists, painters, poets, and playwrights. Some of these eggs range from Lu Xun's *Kuangren riji* ("The Diary of a Madman," 1918), Liu Bang Nong's (Liu Fu) famous love poem *Jiao Wo Ruhe Bu Xiang Ta* ("Help me to know how I cannot think of her," 1926), Ch'ien Chung-shu's novel *Wei Cheng* (*Fortress Besieged*, 1946), to the 2002 short film "Bus 44" (*Che Si Shi Si*). All of which are illustrative of only "some" of the eggs, rather than "all" of the eggs.

These are some of the eggs, which, as earlier mentioned, may be good and bad eggs, good or bad eggs, similarly shaped-eggs or differently shaped-eggs, and the same or different kinds of eggs. Just as a sampling of some of the eggs lead us to know that Chinese culture is a wealth of diversity, rich in meanings, and continues to link strongly to Chinese history, philosophies, and different schools of thought.

For these reasons, the book is about Chinese culture, the Chinese family system, and the Chinese people. It is about the culture and people that Lin Yutang, in his classic, *My*

Just "Making Life"

County and My People (1998), essentially describes as the real Chinese people. When addressing the longevity and potency of Chinese culture, as Lin (1998) earlier observed, "Young China, being wearied of the revolutionary ardors of its fathers, is going back to old China. It is almost amusing to see the often self-conscious determination to be really Chinese, to eat Chinese food, to live in Chinese ways, to dress in Chinese clothes."

What all of this, ultimately, says about Chinese culture is that the old is new again, as Chinese culture continues to regenerate itself throughout the generations to come. In the context of both old and modern China, a befitting quote reads, "There is no new thing under the sun" (*Bible*, Ecclesiastes 1: 9). The fact that the old is new again is a reality that even Mao Zedong also took to heart, when he astutely observed, "Time changes, and men and women are the same," but actually, and impliedly, time changes, and nothing changes.

All of this also presents question of whether the West should learn more about Chinese culture, in order to more effectively engage China. This is because, in many of the critical aspects of life, society, politics, and economics, we ought to emulate many of China's successes. The reasons are many such as the Chinese philosopher or Confucian Mengzi (Mencius) earlier, during Chinese antiquity, advocating, "Rule a big country as you would fry a small fish." Then in a more recent example, there is the former Singapore Prime Minister Lee Kuan Yew advising the United States to co-op Southeast Asian countries into its system via free trade agreements, while it has the bigger market, lest suffer the consequence of these countries drifting to China, which is where the real profits are.

In answer to the question, which was earlier set forth in the Preface – If you ask who the real Chinese people are? It is about Chinese culture, the Chinese family system, and a Chinese people that were able to survive disasters and re-generate themselves from one disaster to the next. These are the real Chinese people, who simply want to "make life" (*weile shenghuo*). Therefore, in the end, If you ask who the real Chinese people are?, you will find the real Chinese people just simply trying to "make life."

Bibliography

Abrams, M. H. 1984. *Structure and Style in the Greater Romantic Lyric, The Correspondent Breeze: Essays on English Romanticism*, New York: Norton.

Albanese, Catherine. 1966. "Religion and American Popular Culture: An Introductory Essay," in *Journal of the American Academy of Religion* 64:4, 733-742.

Alford, William P. and Fang Liufang. 1994. Legal Training and Education in the 1990s: An Overview and Assessment of China's Needs, Report for the World Bank, 16 (1994), pp. 39.

Alighieri, Dante. c1305. "De Vulgari Eloquentia" (On Elegance in the Vernacular, In ed. P.V. Mengaldo, *Opere minori II*, Milan: R. Riccciardi, 1979, 26-237; (Treatise on the origin and function of natural languages).

Barnhart, Richard, M. 1996. *Li Kung-Lins "Classic of Filial Piety"* (Metropolitan Museum of Art Publications), Harry N. Abrams, Inc.

Bodde, Derk. 1946. "Dominant Ideas in the Formation of Chinese Culture," *JAOS*, 62, (December 1942), 233-9. Reprinted in *Harvard Educational Review*, 13 (March1943), 127-139. Reprinted with slight changes in Harley F. McNair, ed., *China* (United Nations Series, Berkeley & Los Angeles: University of California Press, 1946), p. 18-20.

Cai Xiqin (trans). 1994. *Analects of Confucius.*

Cao, Xueqin, E. Gao, Xianyi Yang, and Gladys Yang. 2001. *A Dream of a Red Mansion*, Beijing: Foreign languages press.

Cao, Zuoya. 1998. *The Internal and the External: A Comparison of the Artistic Use of Natural Imagery in English Romantic and Chinese Classic Poetry*, New York: Peter Lang.

Carroll, Robert and Stephen Prickett. 2008. *The Bible: Authorized King James Version* (Oxford World's Classics), Oxford University Press, USA.

Chidester, David. 1996. "The Church of Baseball, the Fetish of Coca-Cola, and the Potlatch of Rock 'n' Roll," *J Am Acad Relig*, Vol. LXIV, Iss. 4, pp. 743-765.

Ch'ien, Chung-shu. 1946. *Wei Cheng*, trans. By Jeanne Kelly and Nathan K. Mao, Beijing: The People's Literature Publishing House, December; [*Fortress Beseiged*].

Bibliography

China's basic old-age pension payment to reach 400 billion yuan, *China Daily*, Dec. 15. 2005.

Confucius, and D. C. Lau. 1979. *The Analects*, Harmondsworth: Penguin Books.

De Bary, William Theodore. 1998. *Asian Values and Human Rights: A Confucian Communitarian Perspective*, Cambridge, Mass: Harvard University Press, p. 120.

Devarajan, Arthi and Harshita Mruthinti Kamath. 2009. "Victory of a Dream: Reimagining *The Nutcracker* in Classical Indian Dance," in *Practical Matters*, January, Vol. 1, No. 1, pp. 1-20.

Ding, Naifei. 2002. *Obscene Things: Sexual Politics in Jin Ping Mei*, Durham: Duke University Press.

Durkheim, Emile. 1951. *Suicide, a Study in Sociology*, [1897], Glencoe, IL: Free Press; [*Le Suicide*].

_____. 1938. *The Rules of Sociological Method*, New York: Free Press, p. xlix.

Eaton, Jana S. 1998. "Gender Issues in Transitional China," *Multicultural Education*," Winter.

Edwards, Louise. 2003. "Ding Naifei, Obscene Things: Sexual Politics in Jin Ping Mei," Durham: Duke University Press, 2002, Review by Louise Edwards, *Intersections: Gender, History and Culture in the Asian Context*, Issue 9, August.

Emerson, John K. 1985. *A View from Yenan*, Washington, D.C.: Institute for the Study of Diplomacy, Edmund A. Walsh School of Foreign Service, Georgetown University.

Evslin, Bernard. 1980. *The Adventures of Ulysses*, Scholastic Paperbacks, Reissue edition.

Feng, Menglong, et al. 1981. The Courtesan's Jewel Box: Chinese Stories of the Xth-XVIIth Centuries, (1957) (Yang Hsien-yi, trans. and Gladys Yang, trans.), Beijing: Foreign Languages Press.

Fu, Jing. 2005. More Capital to Tackle Pension Deficit, *China Daily*, March 28.

Fung, Yu-lan. 1991. *Selected Philosophical Writing of Fung Yu-Lan*, Beijing: Foreign Language Press.

_____1952. *A History of Chinese Philosophy*. Volume I: The Period of the Philosophers (From the Beginnings to circa 100 B.C.). Princeton: Princeton University Press, p. 295.

Gao, Xingjiang. 2000. (Nobel Lecture), "The case for literature," trans. Mabel Lee, The Nobel Prize in Literature 2000 © THE NOBEL FOUNDATION 2000; Nobelrpize.org,http://nobelprize.org/literature/laureates/2000/gao-lecture-e.html.

Gernet, Jacques. 1996. *A History of Chinese Civilization*, Cambridge University Press, 2nd ed., pp. 13-18.M.

Graves Robert. 1993. *The Greek Myths*, Penguin, Reprint edition.

Bibliography

Gu, Zhizhong. 2001. *Creation of the Gods*, (Library of Chinese Classics: Chinese-English: Four Volumes), Beijing: Foreign Language Press; [*Fengsheng Yanyi*].

Greenspan, Alan. 2007. (Alan Greenspan Interview), Meet the Press Transcript for September 23, 2007, Unpublished;http://www.msnbc.msn.com/id/20941413/page/4/.

He, Zhaowu, et. al. 1991. *An Intellectual History of China*, He Zhaowu trans., pp. 15-16.

Holden, Stephen. 1996. (Movie Review), "Temptress Moon (1996) – A 'Gone With the Wind' In China, Without War," *The New York Times*, October 5.

Hu, Shi. 1934. *The Chinese Renaissance: The Haskell lectures*, Chicago: University of Chicago Press.

Jennings, William. 1969. *The Shi King: The Old "Poetry Classic" of the Chinese*, New York: Paragon Book.

Jian, Xu. 2011. "A criticism of Lin Yutang's translation on Tao-te Ching, Chapter 1," 2005-201, (Last accessed 6/23/2011);http://www.woodcarvingpainting.com/index34.html.

Jin, Wenxue. 2004. *Koshoku to Chugoku bunka: Chugoku no rekishi wa yoru ni tsukurareta*, Kawaguchi-shi, Japan: Nihon Kyohosha; [English translations: *Erotic History of China and Chinese culture was made at night* or *Chinese culture and sensuality - Chinese history was made at night*].

Karlgren, Bernhard. 1950. *The Book of Odes*, Stockholm: The Museum of Far Eastern Antiquities.

Killion, Ulric. 2006. *A Modern Chinese Journey to the West: Economics Globalization and Dualism*, New York: Nova Science Publishing.

Kohn, Livia. 1991. *Taoist Mystical Philosophy: The Scripture of Western Ascension.* Albany: State University of New York Press.

Kvam, Kristen E., Schearing, Linda S., and Ziegler, Valerie H (Eds.), 1998). *Eve and Adam: Jewish, Christian, and Muslim Readings on Genesis and Gender*, Indiana University Press, Bloomington IN.

Legge, James. 1994. *The Chinese Classics*, Vol. IV, Taipei: SMC Publishing, Inc., Taipei; [The She King].

_____. 1967. *Li Chi: The Book of Rites, an Encyclopedia of Ancient Ceremonial Usages, Religious Creeds, and Social Institutions.* Translated by James Legge, New York: University Books.

Li, Yu. 1963. *Yv Pu Tuan*, Martin; [*Jou Pu Tuan* or *The Prayer Mat of Flesh*].

Lin, Cunxin. 2005. "The Invisible Silence in History—A Gender Study of Lienv Zhuan The Invisible Silence in History—A Gender Study of Lienv Zhuan," *Journal of China Women's College*, Issue: January; [*Zhonghua Nuvi Xueyuan Xuebao*].

Lu, Xun. 1991. "The Arts and Revolution" (Wenyi yu geming), in *The Collected Works of Lu Xun (Lu Xun Quanji)*, Vol.4, Beijing: Renmin Wenxue Chubanshe, p. 84.

Bibliography

_____. 1972. "Kuangren riji," 1918, in *Selected Stories of Lu Hsun*, Beijing: Published by Foreign Languages Press; ["The Diary of a Madman"].

Lin, Yutang. 1998. *My Country and My People*, (1935), Beijing: Foreign Language Teaching and Research Press.

Mahoney, Brian. 2011. "Emotional Rodman caps Hall of Fame Ceremony," *Associated Press*, August 13.

Mair, Victor H. 2002. "Sound and Meaning in the History of Characters: Views of China's Earliest Script Reformers," in *Difficult characters: interdisciplinary studies of Chinese and Japanese writing*, edited by Mary S. Erbaugh. 105-123. National East Asian Languages Resources Center, Ohio State University.

Martin, Richard 1963. *Jou Pu Tuan*, 1 volume, 20 chapters, trans. Richard Martin from the German translation by Franz Kuhn, New York: Grove Press, 1963; [*The Prayer Mat of Flesh*]. The Before-Midnight Scholar, (1 volume, 20 chapters) (trans. Richard Martin from the German translation by Franz Kuhn), (Andre Deutsch, London, 1965).

Mitchell, Margaret. 1993. *Gone With The Wind*, (1936), Warner Books; Reprint edition, August 1.

Morrison, Kenneth. 2006. *Marx, Durkheim, Weber: Formations of Modern Social Thought*, Sage Publications, p. 196.

Nye, Joseph S., Jr. 1991. *Bound to Lead: The Changing Nature of American Power*, Basic Books.

Oxford University Press (China) Ltd. 1999. *Concise English-Chinese, Chinese-English dictionary*. Hong Kong: Oxford University Press (China).

Phan, Pamela N. 2005. "Clinical Legal Education in China: In Pursuit of a Culture of Law and a Mission of Social Justice," Vol. 8, *Yale Human Rights & Development L. J.*, 117, 127.

Pound, Ezra. 1954. *The Classic Anthology Defined by Confucius*, Cambridge: Harvard University Press.

Pu, Songling. 1880. *Strange Stories from a Chinese Studio*, (Translation by Herbert A. Giles), London: T. De La Rue.

Shakespeare, William. 2007. *Complete Works of William Shakespeare* (New Library Collection), Wordsworth.

Shih, June. 2003. Ford Foundation, From the Rule of Man to the Rule of Law, ¶ 12, (Last accessed May 18, 2011); http://www.fordfound.org/publications/ff_report/view _ff_report_detail.cfm?report_index=431.

Stanton, Elizabeth Cady. 1896. *Free Thought Magazine*, Vol. 114, p. 1.

Roy, David Todd (trans.). 2001. "The Plum in the Golden Vase, or Chin P'ing Mei," Volume 2, *The Rivals*, Princeton University Press, October 1.

_____. 1997. "The Plum in the Golden Vase or, Chin P'ing Mei," Volume 1, *The Gathering*, Princeton University Press; Reprint edition, March 17.

Bibliography

Rubin, Vitaly Aronovich. 1982. "Editor's Note," in *Journal of Chinese Philosophy* 9 (2):267-267.

Sima, Qian. 2007. *Ssuma Ch'ien: Including History of the Hsia Dynasty and Yin Dynasty*, Forgotten Books.

Sun Tzu. 1963. *The Art of War*, trans. Samuel B. Griffith, London: Oxford University Press.

Tang, Tao. 1998. *History of Modern Chinese Literature*, Beijing: Foreign Languages Press, p. 27.

Vitiello, Giovanni. 2003. "Obscene Things: Sexual Politics in Jin Ping Mei" (Review), *China Review International*, Vol. 10, No. 1, 139-143, Spring, University of Hawaii Press.

Wong, Yin Lee. 1975. "Women's Education in Traditional and Modern China," *Women's History Review*, Vol. 4, No. 3, November 3.

Xin, Guanjie. 1994. *Analects of Confucius*, Translation by Cai Xiqin, Beijing: 1994.

Xu, Jiang-hong. 2005. "Lun Bai-Tuan-Da-Zhan De Lish Yiyi" [The Historical Significance of Bai-Turan–Da-Zhan], *Guihai Lun Cong* [Guihai Tribune], Naning, Guangxi, China: Guangxi Zhuang Autonomous Region Party, May.

Yan, Jinfen. 2002. "A Feminine Expression of Mysticism, Romanticism and Syncretism in A Plaint of Lady Wang," *Inter-Religio* 42, Winter, pp. 3-20.

Yang, Yixian et al. 2001. *The Book of Songs*, Beijing: The Foreign Language Press.

Yang Bojun. 1958. *Lunyu Yizhu*, Beijing: Zhonghua shuju.

Ye, Yonglie. 1993. *Jiang Qing zhuan*, Beijing, pp. 607-08; [*Biography of Jiang Qing*].

_____, 1992. "Jiang Qing: Cong Shanghai dao Yan'an," in *Haishang wentan* 11 (September/October), pp. 4-23; ["Jiang Qing: From Shanghai to Yan'an"].

Yuan, Zhong Xu (trans.), and Sheng Zhang Jiang (ed.). 1993. *Shi Jing*, Jiang, Hunan, China: Hu Nan Chu Ban She.

Zhang, Rulun. 2005. "Independence and Self-Consciousness of Chinese Philosophy: On the Rewriting of the History of Chinese Philosophy," *Social Sciences in China* (Zhongguo shehui kexue), Spring, pp. 28-29.

Zhao, Dunhua. 2005. "Introduction to Special Isssue: Contemporary China's Philosophy: From Dialogue to Innovation," *Social Sciences in China* (Zhongguo shehui kexue), Spring, pp. 110-111.

Index

Index

Index

Index

Index

Index

About The Author

The author has traveled extensively throughout Asia, while also for many years living in the People's Republic of China. He has lectured on various subjects or areas of law and law and economics at American, British, and Chinese universities. He also has authored several books, book chapters, and journal publications, including Modern Chinese Rules of Order: Paradox of Law and Economics, and A Modern Chinese Journey to the West: Economic Globalization and Dualism.